The Spirit of Holiness

The
SPIRIT
of
HOLINESS

by Everett Lewis Cattell
President, Malone College
Canton, Ohio

William B. Eerdmans Publishing Company
Grand Rapids, Michigan

First printing, February 1963
Second printing, December 1964

PHOTOLITHOPRINTED BY GRAND RAPIDS BOOK MANUFACTURERS, INC.
GRAND RAPIDS, MICHIGAN
PRINTED IN THE UNITED STATES OF AMERICA

TO

MOTHER

Preface

It has been my happy privilege for many years, both in America and in India, to preach across the lines that divide Christians in their views of the deeper spiritual life. This book contains the gist of what I have preached, now from one passage of Scripture and now from another.

I was brought up in the Friends Church with its traditional emphasis upon the work of the Holy Spirit. During the last hundred years large sections of American Quakerism have been deeply influenced by the Wesleyan emphasis of the National Holiness Association of America. Hence, I was brought up on "holiness." As a young Christian trying to live the sanctified life, I found problems in correlating the teaching I heard with my own experience. This drove me to a deeper study of the actual teaching.

Here I found that much confusion was being caused by the fact that the Holiness movement was emphasizing certain truths or facets of truth to the neglect or near exclusion of others. For example, the valid truth about crisis experience had been so emphasized as to leave the development of the holy life neglected. The average preacher was out in every sermon to catch one more soul for the crisis — and showed little concern for the multitude who had passed through the crisis and needed help in going on from there to the living out of the holy life. Another weakness was the failure to distinguish between the carnal nature to be eradicated and the purified human nature which needs to be disciplined. Many were afraid of discipline for fear of being guilty of "suppression." Nor was temptation in the life of holiness given adequate treatment.

By studying the writings of the really responsible leaders in the movement and particularly by going back to Wesley himself, I found the answers to these questions given, but usually tucked away out of the light of major emphasis. Moreover, I found that the doctrine of holiness squared better with Scripture when it was kept in balance. And so I began to preach with an effort to clarify the confusions I had experienced. The result, as it has developed over the years, is contained in the following pages.

Before I went to India I had only slight association with people in the Victorious Life movement, but nevertheless I came to feel that the differences between "Holiness" and "Victorious Life" were more a matter of definition than of reality. In India I met, perforce, all kinds of people. We missionaries, thank God, are not able to live in the splendid denominational isolation of the West. As doors for ministry opened to groups of varying background, I was driven to a more Scriptural and elemental expression of truth than is required in a circle where shibboleths reign. I have tried to understand what differing views of the deeper spiritual life, or life of holiness, really are, and to give a clear statement of what I believe all views have in common.

It remains for the reader to discover whether this presentation is helpful or not. I am impressed from study that life in the Spirit is hard to express, just because it is life. Words, at best, are "frozen thought" and inadequate fully to express life. Even the Apostle Paul struggled to find adequate language for the paradoxes he experienced. It is therefore of the essence of bigotry for any of us to claim finality for our way of expressing the deeper spiritual life. May God help us past words to the reality of what Phillips calls "the holiness which is no illusion" (Eph. 4:24).

—EVERETT LEWIS CATTELL

Canton, Ohio

Contents

1

The Time Element in Salvation

My father told me that "tomorrow is always coming but never arrives." This puzzled me as a boy and I pondered long on how it could be that tomorrow always stayed in the future. When it arrives it becomes today. Years later I learned that boys are not alone in being puzzled by time. Philosophers write large books to summarize their thoughts about it. What gives to time its element of continuity? Where is the past? Whence comes the future? All we know of the past is in memory. What we know of the future is in imagination. And what gives the present its special character of fluidity? It is easier to ask these questions than to answer them.

We have learned to divide time into past, present, and future. The really important part of time for us is the vital, living, fluid moment which we call *now*. How long is *now*? Looked at in one way it is a mere instant. In another way we can say that we have never lived any time but *now*, for every moment we have ever lived was a *now* moment. *Now* is therefore a great continuum — something more than the memory of past moments — and that is why we feel that the *now* is qualitatively different from past and future time — it seems to be the point at which Eternity breaks into the time stream, like a live coal passing through a draft of air, to glow with a brightness all its own. That is *now*. As we

11

move along in time we live only in the *now*, for it moves with us. That is what the Apostle means when he says, "Now is the day of salvation." Not only is *now* the time for decision for Christ but the only salvation having any validity or significance is that which goes with us moment by moment. That is the sense in which John so often speaks of us "*having*" eternal life. This is what Paul meant in Romans 8:1 when he says, "There is therefore *now* no condemnation." It is not enough that we point back to the day we were reconciled to God and born anew. It is necessary that we live without condemnation each succeeding moment of the *now*.

While driving a car one very frequently comes upon new road construction the focal point of which is a concrete mixer. It is pouring out a fluid mass which workmen are molding to a satisfactory surface. This is the *now*. Stretching back from this lies perhaps miles of "white ribbon" highway: former *nows* which have crystallized into memory. Ahead lies a stretch of cut ground and concrete forms: imagination, an engineer's vision, hope. But the crucial point is the mixer, the fluid *now*.

Salvation is, more than anything else, a matter of the present moment; a living, fluid, formative thing. It has its memories and its hopes, but these become escapes from reality if made substitutes for the salvation that is *now*.

Christian experience has its memories. There is, for instance, the memory of conversion wonderfully expressed for us in the hymn,

> *O happy day that fixed my choice*
> *On Thee, my Saviour and my God.*

Happy is the man who can point back to a definite time when his crisis occurred — when he became a Christian. In a normal human birth no one ever thinks he is doing injustice to the long period of pre-natal development already undergone, nor to the long schooling yet to come by making quite a crisis event of the actual birth. The mother knows that day is special and the father rarely goes through it un-moved. All are agreed it is worth making records about and celebrating annually thereafter. Why should it be different with spiritual rebirth? There may be evangelistic methods which neglect pre-natal care, result in still-births, or which leave the baby to perish by the roadside. But the cure for this is not to try to omit the simple fact of birth!

There are other crises in our dealings with the Lord: victories won, prayers answered, guidance received, the Word illuminated, and witness given and made fruitful. For all these we thank God, and perhaps most of all for the one where we surrendered our wills utterly to Him and received His cleansing and that purity of heart which made holy living possible.

The Christian, then, is enriched by the memories of spir-itual crises. He must guard immediately, however, against any *memory* becoming an escape from facing the challenge of the living *now*. I have in mind those testimonies in which one hears again and again references made to a conversion experience in terms of month, day and hour, and a spot grown dear, all of which is ground for rejoicing, except that one detects a barrenness in it all because salvation as a con-tinuing process is neglected. Salvation is a memory. Such folk cannot testify that *"now* is the day of salvation" with them. Did not John Wesley rule for his class meetings that in them no testimony should be given that was more than a week old? What a difference this would make in our witness today.

Hope is likewise a blessed part of the divine grace when used as an enrichment of present experience of Christ, but it is a deep peril when made an escape from present reality. Imagination is the home of invention, but also of daydream-ing. It is the stuff out of which ideals of service are wrought, and also escapes from reality. Multitudes of Christians cover their life of inner defeat with hope in the form of promises to themselves that *someday* they will come to grips with and get the victory over this besetting sin or that bad habit or this other recurring failure.   They need to remember that salvation is *now*!

Christianity is a religion of hope. "If in this life only we have hope in Christ, we are of all men most miserable" (I Cor. 15:19).   It is noteworthy that historically the doctrine of Christian hope has flourished in direct proportion to the amount of suffering men were having to endure. Some of us, however, are grateful that our hope is not the outgrowth of suffering but of believing steadily a "more sure word of prophecy." We have hope because of the Word of God.   But this glorious hope must not be an escape from reality *now*!   To the Christian, hope is a force with which he nerves the daily endeavor. It is essentially unchristian to use this hope as an escape from facing today's challenge. Any emphasis upon the return of our Lord which relieves us of responsibility for trying to change our present evil society is an unworthy escape.

Salvation as a present, living, vital matter must be rooted in the Cross. The Cross of sublime memory is not enough. It must become a part of our present, living moment of experience.   It is easy to sing about glorying in the Cross of Christ which towers above the wrecks of time, and all the while refuse to take it up for today's walk.   We have too many decorative crosses: stained glass windows, cruciform cathedrals, jewelry, and the like.   Beautiful crosses!   But without sweat, and dirt, and blood, and agony.   Gaylord B. Noyce suggested that the Cross has become so idealized that to preserve its offense we had better use a noose instead! We need the Cross as a way of living experience in the salvation that is *now*!

The Cross enters our Christian experience at the point where we surrender our efforts to impress God with our goodness and kneel to receive the forgiveness of our sins, being reconciled with Him through the offering of Christ's blood.   This is the objective Cross. It appears again when we yield ourselves a living sacrifice unto God. It persists as we face the world and the things that are in the world. So long as there is an unsaved man in the world, and so long as Christ's kingdom does not cover the earth as the waters cover the sea, so long will the true Christian carry the Cross in his heart. This is the subjective Cross. Both the subjective and objective phases of the Cross are essential to the salvation that is *now*.

Waste no pity on the truly surrendered Christian who has taken the way of the Cross in seriousness, for he is the happiest man in the world. He has found his home at last. Life has become transformed in a moment and the transformation abides as a continuing thing, provided he keeps his experience of Christ in the *now*. He has learned the secret of abiding. Here is a glorious privilege. It is on this level that life becomes radiant, joyous, and miraculous. The folk to be pitied are those who are merely religious, having never gone the whole way of surrender to the will of God, having never clasped the Cross.

Salvation that has in it the glow of the living present depends, then, upon nothing so much as upon Christ Himself, crucified and risen, entering into us and we into Him. When one has experienced this kind of salvation he can never be content with less. Just as the church must continually battle against the stifling encroachment of formalism upon its spiritual life, so the individual Christian must ever be on his guard against sagging from that level of salvation which is living, glowing, glorious and real — and all that, *now*!

How can we preserve the glow? What should we do when we find our experience slipping to humdrum levels again? Sometimes we become aware that although there has been no conscious break in our fellowship with God, no choice of sin, yet there is less of joy, of adventure, of glow in our experience than previously. What can be done about it? How can we keep a sense of miracle in our Christian life?

First, we should check on our relationships with others. *Righteousness* and *love* are the tests. If we have wronged another and made no redress, it is folly to hope for the salvation that is *now*. Our relationships must be *right*. This means returning property that belongs to others, correcting wrong impressions we have given, and keeping our promises both to God and man.

In one of my pastorates there was a man who was often in the slough of despair. He could not seem to keep any glow in his experience. One Sunday night after meeting he confessed to me that the trouble was that he always promised God to make certain restitutions but in fact never did. We agreed then to set out the next morning together and not come back until he kept his promises. First, there was the street railway company to settle with for rides stolen when he was a boy. There was also a steam railway company upon the back end of whose trains he once or twice rode several hundred miles without a ticket. (It was interesting to observe the difficulty in these companies to decide just which officer was competent to handle such cases.) So far the offenses were gladly forgiven. Then we hunted for a long time throughout the city for an old Jew, a retired junk dealer. Back during the first World War my friend as one of a party of eight young men climbed the fence of the junk yard at night, stole a cartload of old iron, and the next morning wheeled it in and re-sold it to the Jew. They bought liquor with the money. Tears streamed down the old Jew's face as he heard our story. It did him so much good, he said, to see an honest man. He was a millionaire — through junk — and didn't want the money, but if the man wanted to clear his conscience he could give five dollars to the preacher who could give it to some widow for shoes for her children. It was done. Then there were doctor bills of several years' standing and other accounts long overdue and given up as bad debts by the creditors. And in the end, such peace and joy! Vital salvation must be based on *righteousness*.

My wife once told this story to a group of Indian Christians and one of the leaders felt deeply convicted for having often traveled on trains without a ticket, which on Indian trains is very easy to do. Encouraged by the story of how one man was so quickly forgiven he went promptly to the Divisional Traffic Manager, confessed his ticketless travel and said that as a Christian he wanted to make it right. The D.T.M. immediately inquired the number of times and the stations between which the rides occurred, calculated the fares, and presented a bill. The Christian leader soon came telling my wife about it and saying, "What's this now? I thought you said the man was freely forgiven when he apologized — and here I have to pay this bill!" Righteousness does not come cheap!

It is not the size of the matter that counts — it is little foxes that spoil the vine of a clear conscience. It onetime took settlement for an unpaid merry-go-round ride in an amusement park to get my boyish soul clear.

Not only righteousness but also *love* is a test in our relationships. It may be that in the work of the church we have taken a stand for the right which has involved us in a relationship badly lacking in love. The quicker we get the matter clear, the better it will be, for suspicion and tension have a tendency to rapid growth. I am sure that ninety-nine per cent of the quarrels in churches arise not from evil motives but from misunderstanding. "A lack of understanding usually leads to misunderstanding." Being a Christian means living a transparent life and keeping all our relationships transparent. Immense defeat comes from insisting that the trouble is with the other party and that therefore nothing can be done about it. No matter how right I have been, I am under obligation as a Christian to recognize that if my brother hath ought against me I am thereby party to a wrong relationship, and I cannot claim that I am living in love with all men until I have taken the *initiative* in a thorough effort at settlement. If I wait for my brother to take the initiative, I share the guilt. Loving frankness is a Christian grace that ought to be more amply cultivated in our day.

A second test for vital Christian living is the matter of

victory over temptation. There is probably no quicker
way to lose the glow than to walk the path of defeat. Perhaps defeat has become so much the rule that one now feels
much less compunction than formerly, and, indeed, has
thought up some good reasons why he could not be expected to do better. One may even have consecrated his
life to mission work in a distant land and still harbor these
inner defeats. The test of absolute surrender to God nine
times out of ten concerns not a spectacular thing like leaving
home for the mission field, but rather forsaking that pet sin
which always bobs up accusingly. Can we hope for nothing
better than a way of defeat from the perfect Christ? Must
we tell of being saved ten years ago and harbor up-to-date
memories of defeat? No, thank God, we can be "more
than conquerors through him that loved us." When the
Cross becomes real enough in our own hearts to become the
crucifixion spot for those very sins which defeat us, we shall
experience the resurrection power of the Living Christ in a
salvation which is *now,* full of glow and *victory.* This is the
essence of sanctification. Sanctification is a crisis experience
in that one arrives at a moment of all-inclusive surrender,
and it is a process in that it involves carrying the validity of
that surrender into every succeeding moment of the eternal
now, applying it to additional areas of un-Christlike living
within us as they are revealed by the abiding Christ who is the
Holy Spirit.

Closely akin to the maintenance of victory is the *discipline
of the devotional life.* It is a glorious privilege that we are
able in an instant and in a noisy crowd to lift our hearts
in prayer with assurance that God hears. But this is a poor
substitute for those longer periods of quiet devotion in
which we talk with God and He speaks to us and in which
the soul finds dimensions.

Hop, skip and jump devotions produce trifling character.
There is positively no substitute for quiet and for medita-
tion if one wants depth of character. There is no correc-
tive for shallow and shifting philosophies like the reading

of the Word of the Eternal God. There is no way to ex-
pedite the day's work and to increase one's personal efficiency
comparable to listening each morning to God in moments
when we hold our peace. And there is no such sure way
to change things as to pray.

I was conducting services once in a large girls' high school
and training college in India. The staff arranged a day
when I was to grant personal interviews to any desiring
them. The students came by the dozen. And the question
which headed the list was, What to do with wandering
thoughts in prayer? American apartment house dwellers
will be able to sympathize with the girls, in that part of
their inability to concentrate was due to inability to get
privacy. I was glad to tell them, first, that wandering
thoughts in prayer are not sin; second, that these have to
be handled just like wandering thoughts while studying
school lessons — by training ourselves to concentrate; and,
third, that to open the devotional period with Bible reading instead of prayer would help to collect one's thoughts.
Discipline need not be bondage. It should be the path to
a higher freedom. To a few people the devotional life is a
compelling delight. To most of us it must first be a
discipline.

Whenever my soul is getting lean I always check up at
once to see whether, first, I have been praying definitely and,
second, whether I have been receiving definite answers to
prayer. For indefinite praying always gets indefinite results.

Finally, I should mention *witnessing* as a means of keeping the glow in Christian experience. Witnessing is not
arguing. I used to get a thrill of self-satisfaction when, with
fellow university students, I found I could hold my own
arguing an evangelical faith. But nobody got converted
by it. Whenever I find myself arguing religion with any
one now, I know I am failing. In witnessing there is no
argument. It is sharing, and if the thing you share is not
real it is false witnessing. Witnessing to one of another
faith, as to Jews or Hindus or Mohammedans, makes you

search your heart, and the bringing forth and putting into words of something real from your experience of Christ brings in its wake new assurance of reality. It tends to crystallize for one his own knowledge of inner resources. In addition to being a most effective method for winning men to Christ, it exerts a reflexive influence of great value.

By these and many other means one holds and cultivates the salvation which is in the living *now*.

2

The Sanctification of Self

The Holy Spirit is given to the redeemed person at his conversion. It is proper, however, to distinguish this from what is often referred to as the "fulness of the Spirit." What is meant by the "fulness of the Spirit" is that He now fully possesses us. We only have Him in fullness when He fully controls us. Theoretically and Scripturally there is no reason why this could not happen simultaneously with conversion, but in actual practice it seems for nearly everyone to happen later. This receiving of the Holy Spirit is expressed by Paul in Romans 5:5, "The love of God is shed abroad in our hearts by the Holy Ghost which is given unto us."

I was preaching from this text once under very uninspiring circumstances. The Christmas holidays were over and we evangelists were back in camp. It was rainy and cold as we sat on the mud floor of an Indian mud-walled house, trying to have a Sunday morning worship service. There were less than a dozen of us. We had just passed through some bitter experiences of rejection, and everyone felt something less than inspired, if not positively low. I was trying to bring a little message from the Word when suddenly came one of those experiences, which preachers understand, of being given something from above. It was a thought about the expression "shed abroad." Of course God is love and so shedding His love abroad is synonymous with shedding abroad Himself in the person of His Holy Spirit. But shedding abroad is a term best figured in light. Press the button, the bulb is illuminated, and instantly light is shed abroad throughout the room. So far as the light is concerned it is ready instantly to occupy every nook and corner of the room. The only reason for its not arriving is the presence of things which cast shadows — boxes, furniture, people and the like.

Then I pictured to my Indian friends a *Diwali* preparation. This is a Hindu holiday in the fall after the rains have stopped. It is preceded by a thorough house cleaning, fresh whitewashing and decorating with lights. I reminded them of how boxes and furniture and all movable things are put out of a room before it is swept and whitewashed. I told them also of the boxes and furniture and things that clutter up our hearts and cast shadows and keep the Holy Spirit from penetrating to the corners so that He might occupy in fullness. These things I labeled jealousy and bitterness and wrath and evil-speaking and gossip and standing up for your family members when they are wrong, the love of money, and the like.

I do not think my picture made much impression on the preachers — it was too simple and not very theological — but there was a village man present who listened, for a change, with rapt attention. Although he was a recent convert, he was not altogether satisfactory. He had fixed his eyes on other Christians and their shortcomings. He was both jealous and bitter over their preferment in jobs and positions in the church. Much of his feeling had grown to ugly proportions.

For some weeks after my preaching I did not know just what had happened that morning. The fact was that this simple villager had a house cleaning. He could not have labeled it theologically nor have given a very satisfactory testimony about it. But the cleansing was real. Weeks later we were talking together as a group about the fullness of the Spirit when suddenly light dawned and he told us that this was what had happened to him that Sunday morning. And, as we observed, the change in his life from that Sunday morning was as marked as it had been at his conversion.

It is not enough that we should receive the Holy Spirit. We must have Him in fullness — He must have us fully. He is not holding out on us. He does not have to be begged and coaxed to come in. Long seasons of groaning and struggling are not necessary to make Him willing to enter. Jesus' word for it is: "Behold, I stand at the door, and knock: if any man hear my voice, and open the door, I will come in to him" (Rev. 3:20). He stands and knocks at our heart's door. It is impossible to ignore Him with impunity. To fail to open the door is to refuse Him. That is disastrous. But if we open — He comes! It is not written, "If any man struggle, or cry, or plead, or labor to be good," — no: "If any man hear my voice, and open the door." It is as simple as that. He is as ready to fill us instantly with His Spirit as light is ready to occupy every corner of a room in which it is shed abroad.

If there is any delay, any struggle, any begging and coaxing, it is due, not to His unwillingness but to our difficulty in getting the door open. Roughly speaking the older we grow, the longer we postpone commitment, the dirtier our hearts, the more entrenched our habits, the more difficult it is to open the door. Furthermore, we must not confuse His simple entry in fullness with any particular way we may feel about it. To some folk it is an immense thrill, to others an overmastering emotional tide, while to others it is simple peace. None of this is normative — the essential is simply the cleansing.

My poor old Grandfather first heard of this experience from a man who declared that when the Holy Spirit filled him it struck him like an electric shock going from head to foot. He was sure Grandfather ought to get the shock also. So for six months Grandfather went about seeking for an electric shock which, fortunately, he was unable to get. What a pity it would have been if he had merely gotten a shock! As it was he at last realized that what he needed and wanted was not a shock nor any other phenomena, but just the Holy Spirit Himself.

"If any man hear my voice, and open the door, I will come in to him." It is only our unsurrendered will that can keep Him out, and there need be no further evidence than the witness of His Spirit to our cleansed conscience that the door is open, to claim by faith His promise of entrance. One need not have the testimony of his senses in any phenomenal way to *know* that the Holy Spirit is in the house.

If this be true, then why is it that so many struggle so long before fullness of the Spirit is accomplished? Seeing that the delay is not the fault nor the will of God, we must examine more closely what it is in us that holds Him off. Unfortunately our refusal to open the door is no mere ephemeral mood but rather a consistent state of rebellion. That is an ugly word, but it has to be said because it is true. Sophistication does not change it. Paul says that "the carnal mind is enmity against God" (Rom. 8:7). We sometimes hate to admit it but there are definite areas in which we resent God's interference in our lives. That is the carnal mind.

Paul's fuller explanation is to be found in a lengthy passage in Romans 6, where he uses the master-slave relationship, pointing out that sin may be our master unto death, or righteousness may be our master unto holiness. The choice of masters is ours, but we cannot serve both. "When ye were the servants of sin, ye were free from righteousness." Again and again in the passage he refers to "being made free from sin," and indicates that then and then only can we become the servants of righteousness. So it is which master we acknowledge that determines our being "after the Spirit" or "after the flesh."

In Ephesians Paul talks of the "old man" and the "new man" and thereby further clarifies his meaning. It may help us to think of these as two patterns of life, one revolving around self as center — that is sin (the old man), and the other revolving around God as center — that is holiness

(the new man). All of the events and stuff of which life is
made fall into one or the other of these two patterns. Indeed, in some measure these patterns exist simultaneously
in most incompletely surrendered hearts, overlapping so that,
pictured geometrically, there is an ellipse where a circle
ought to be.

This may be illustrated by passing a horseshoe magnet
under a sheet of paper on which have been sprinkled iron
filings. Looking from above one cannot see the magnet,
but one can tell the location of its poles by the behavior of
the filings, which instantly arrange themselves around the
poles and form two overlapping patterns. In the lives of
converted men there are still two great poles — self and
God. All of the particles that go to make up life group
themselves around these two poles in patterns of life which
are partially self-centered and partially God-centered. It is
conceivable that the particles where the patterns overlap
have a hard time making up their minds as to which pole
to obey. James has this conflict in mind when he speaks of
the "double minded man" who is "unstable in all his ways."
Now the carnal mind is precisely the mentality whose center
is self, and the pattern it forms in life is displeasing to God
just because it is enmity against Him.

What then is to be done? The Apostle uses strong language. His common terms are "crucify," "mortify," "put
to death," "strip off," and like terms. We must be careful
here to understand correctly. Paul wants the old man crucified. It is this pattern which stands off-center from God,
which must go out of existence as definitely and decisively
as death. But we must be very clear as to just what goes
out of existence and what becomes of it, for it is at this
point that so much misunderstanding has arisen over the
terms "eradication" and "suppression" and "counteraction."
Obviously there is confusion here, for those who object
most strenuously to eradication still insist upon the crucifixion of the old man (which of course is the Scriptural
term), while those who stress eradication are usually no

more certain or clear as to just what it is that is to be eradicated than their opponents are as to what it is that is to be
crucified. It is clear that everyone agrees that *something* has
to be dealt with and eliminated decisively. And of course
there are words and phrases — the "old man," the "carnal
nature," the "sinful nature," the "bias to evil," the "cor-
rupted nature." But what both camps lack is a clear trans-
lation of these terms into language psychologically compre-
hensible so that, in terms of everyday experience, we can
recognize just what is to be eliminated, and what is left, and
what is to be done with what is left.

The answer to the problem lies in the position of the
self. To return to our illustration of the magnet: we saw
a double pattern created by the fact that self stood off-center
from God. Now the crucial point for understanding is that
this doubleness of pattern must go out of existence, but
not the self which is its center. Those who are striving for
the deeper life in the Spirit often call for the death of self.
One realizes what is meant, but nevertheless the language
is inaccurate. The self can never die. It is eternal. It is
the center of the soul and must live forever. God created
it and has no desire that it should be eradicated. It is inaccurate to speak of the death *of* self, but it is entirely proper
to speak of death *to* self. There is a world of difference.
Self must live but *selfishness* must die. There, too, is a
world of difference. Selfishness is that pattern of life which
inevitably results when the self stands apart from God in
any degree. The self as such is holy and good, for it was
made by God. The self is made unholy by choices which
are at variance with God's will.

To show what should be done with the self we need another text. Paul in Colossians 3:3 says: "Ye are dead, and
your life is hid with Christ in God." If we have our difficulties in expressing the deeper life in words, it is some
comfort to realize that Paul himself again and again finds
words failing him as he tries to make it clear. He usually
resorts to paradoxical language. So he does here — "Ye

are dead . . . your life." How can there be life where there
is death? It is a paradox. Something has died. Something
also is very much alive and living on. It may be useful
here to continue our illustration. The self as a pole apart
from God must yield up its aloofness, its separateness, its
enmity against God, its independent sovereignty, by an act
of utter surrender; it must move over and become "hid with
Christ in God." The self then continues to live, but it lives
in God. The poles are now, so to speak, identical, and the
pattern of life is one. This integration, however, cannot
take place without something going out of existence. Not
the self, but the pattern of life created by the self when it
is not hid with Christ in God is the thing that must be destroyed. Now actually this destruction of the "old man" is
difficult only as, and in the measure that, our self-will or enmity toward God is strongly fixed. For some, surrender
appears simple and easy; for others it is a fight. Sometimes
it occurs in an instant of decision; sometimes it occurs only
after long struggle. It never happens by accident. No one
ever just drifts into it. Nothing can be assumed about it.
No mere pious hope will do. Decision is called for. Moreover, surrender must be absolute and final; every last reser-
vation must go. One cannot bargain nor make terms. Paul
uses terms like "crucifixion" and "death" to emphasize the
decisiveness and absoluteness of the action.

These terms, "crucifixion" and "death," are of course
figurative, referring to the pattern and not to the self as
such, and, like all figures of speech, they must not be pressed
beyond their intended use. After they have served to emphasize the way we must deal with the rebellion, we must
drop them. Otherwise we shall get into another common
misunderstanding. For some who have experienced such a
surrender and such a deliverance feel that the carnal nature
is crucified, dead and buried, and that dead things do not
return to bother us. They assume, therefore, that the carnal
nature will never appear again, that there is no use guarding
that front any longer. But Paul never intended his figure

to be pressed to that point. He had finished with it in the moment of full surrender. Then a new figure must be taken up. The self is then "hid with Christ in God." Whatever else this text may mean, it is clear from the context that we have a right to take as its primary meaning its application to the Spirit-filled life. Now the chief weapon of temptation used by the devil against the surrendered and holy heart is to try to draw the self out of its hidden place and, in some particular at least, get it to set up again in independence from God.

The self carries with it all the equipment of human nature with which God endowed us by creation. All of the factors, physical and mental, the drives, urges, instincts (or whatever terms your psychology requires) which are part of normal human nature are instruments controlled by and used for the glory of the dominant center in life. That center may be self-hid-with-Christ-in-God, or self-standing-on-its-own. In the latter case these factors become warped and in ugly fashion reveal the self-centeredness of the life. When they are cleansed, they reveal the glory of God. This is what Paul means when he says that God "shall also quicken your mortal bodies by his Spirit that dwelleth in you" (Rom. 8:11). This means that any of our capacities, our urges, our abilities, physical and mental, all that God made to reside in our bodies, shall, when cleansed, be free from its self-centeredness, its bias to self and evil, its enmity against God, and shall be free, quickened and enlivened, until it shall then really begin to function as God intended it should when He created it. Note that no part of this equipment is to be eliminated, any more than the self is to die. Rather it, like the self, is to be cleansed and hid with Christ in God, where it can at long last function to the glory of God in true holiness as He had originally intended.

George Fox described this very quaintly in his own experience when he said that it seemed as though "all the creation gave another smell unto me than before." This is to say that when enmity against God is cleansed from our hearts our whole being — every sense, every desire, every instinct, every part of our nature — is more sensitive, more alive and more vigorous than ever before, ready now for the first time to be a vessel for the expression of the glory of God.

Upon arrival at a convention in India where I was to preach, I unpacked a new pearl grey suit to wear in the pulpit. To my dismay I found I had left the trousers on a wire hanger throughout the rainy season. There was now a long streak of rust across one leg. This posed a problem: how to remove the rust without, at the same time, taking out the delicate grey color of the suit. There are many chemical substances which could easily have taken out the rust — but they go too far; they would have taken out the color in the cloth and thus have traded a white streak for a rust streak. I am very grateful to a woman who had just the right thing, which took out the rust and left the color as it was originally. Too many views of salvation prescribe cures which would destroy normal human nature along with sin. This we do not want. Thanks be unto God He has provided, through His Son, cleansing which leaves human nature completely intact, including its liability to temptation.

This latter must be recognized as a part of normal human nature — a part of that which God made and saw that it was "good." It is wrong to include our liability to temptation as a part of our fallen or sinful or depraved human nature. The capacity to be tempted is part of our holy moral nature — it was true of Adam and Eve before the fall, and it was true of the sinless Christ. It is not right to bewail our sinful nature just because we are subject to temptation. God wants voluntary love and service, and to get these He made us with the power of choice. This is good, not evil. The sinful nature is the attitude of enmity, and this in turn warps and colors every phase of normal human nature. Until that attitude dies, it is proper to bewail our bias or propensity to evil. Deliverance from enmity against God puts

us on the victory side of temptation, even when it is intensi-
fied by the scars of sin.

For instance, a drunkard may be forgiven and obtain complete victory over his evil habit. But there may still remain
impressed upon the very cells of his body something that
makes the smell of liquor an enticement. Some will call
this his sinful nature. In a broad sense this is possible since
these scars are the result of sin. But we must make a radical
distinction between these scars which are quite involuntary
and amoral now that the past which produced them is forgiven, and that attitude of enmity against the will of God
which is distinctly voluntary, immoral, sinful and to be
legitimately called the sinful nature. If this enmity should
be readmitted to the heart, it will of course find a strong
and probably winning ally in the scar-tissue taste for liquor.

When we speak of deliverance from our sinful nature, it
is necessary to keep this distinction clear. We may be delivered from our inherited attitude of conscious enmity
against God, and that is enough. Moral scars may remain.
Our bodies, our minds, and our spirits may have twists which
will open doors of temptation. But because this persists
for life the case is not hopeless. God's grace is sufficient
to give victory provided we have been delivered from the
root enmity which we consciously harbor until we consciously
and fully surrender it for destruction and cleansing.

In the old days of British rule in India I saw a curious
thing at the investiture ceremony where the Maharajah of
Chhatarpur received, on coming of age, his ruling powers.
The guests were assembled in the Darbar Hall of the Palace
when, with great pomp and ceremony, the Maharajah entered
and occupied one of two thrones at the end of the hall, the
other being occupied by the British Resident. Thus was
symbolized the dual sovereignty under which the Indian
States functioned and which always posed a nice point in
law known as paramountcy. The Maharajah was fully sov-
ereign — and yet within the limits of British paramountcy.
This has its own spiritual lesson, but I am now concerned

with another part of the proceedings. It was that moment when the nobles of the court came to pledge their fealty to the British Crown as they had doubtless done earlier to the Maharajah. Each one in turn came slowly to the throne, bowed low, and extended his hand draped with a silk handkerchief on which was a quantity of gold. It was the right of the Resident on behalf of the Crown to take this gold as a pledge of the loyalty of this Indian nobleman. But instead, he touched it slowly, symbolizing his acceptance of the man's fealty, then withdrew his hand, allowing the man to return to his seat with the gold in his possession. He was free to use that gold in any way he chose so long as it was consistent with his loyalty to the Crown. To use it in any subversive way would be criminal.

Seeing this I was reminded of our crisis experience in which we bring our *all* to King Jesus. He has a right to take it from us, to keep us from misusing it, but that is not His choice. Rather He touches us with the cleansing of His precious blood and then leaves our cleansed human nature in our control as a stewardship. But every use must be consistent with loyalty and such as will glorify Him. He removes from us no particle of our legitimate human nature which He created. He removes only the taint of rebelliousness and purifies our love for Him until it becomes holy obedience.

This truth is so important that it needs to be seen in some detail and we can do so by taking up several items of human nature in turn to see how it works out. In doing so we must see how the devil makes his attacks, and how he tries to worm us out of that hidden place "with Christ in God."

Everyone knows that hunger and eating are essential to life and therefore to the glory of God. Fasting may have value as an ascetic discipline (and certainly for weight reduction) but no one asks for a spiritual experience which would "eradicate" hunger. Still, it is perfectly true that eating to the glory of God and being a glutton are two different things. Where then does one cross the line, in eating,

from the glory of God to gluttony? Obviously, the answer
is not simple. We shall come to that later, but let it suffice
for the present to say that there is a "line" and that eating
on one side of it is consistent with a self-hid-with-Christ-in-
God and on the other side consistent with a self-out-on-its-
own.

Now the solution of this problem does not lie in elimi-
nating the joy from eating. An emotional or feeling tone
accompanies every act we perform. God made us that way
and to try to eradicate feeling is not only impossible but
wrong. The Stoics tried to do so. When a plate of fried
fish was brought before a Stoic he was to stifle his impulse
to say, "Just look at this wonderful meal; I will certainly
enjoy it." Rather he was to say, "See, here is the carcass of
a dead fish; I shall consume it to keep body and soul together." The message of the Bhagavad-Gita runs in the same
vein. But all such teaching ends in hypocrisy or ruin. No,
the Christians' task is more difficult. He is to eat to glorify
God and he is also to enjoy that which is to the glory of God.

I have used this illustration because it is so simple and
because it is universally taken for granted that there is
nothing wrong with the satisfaction of hunger. Yet the
very matter-of-factness with which this is taken for granted
means peril. Why do we hear so few sermons on the sanctification of eating? There are multitudes of overweight
gluttons who claim to be filled with the Spirit to whom it
has never occurred that sanctification has anything to do
with eating. We need to see that hunger, like every other
bit of our human equipment, is a possible servant of self or
of God. Just how this is so will be clearer as we proceed.

Another and less obvious God-given item is sensitiveness.
God made us so that we could feel the sufferings of others
and enter sympathetically into their need. But when sensitiveness is turned in upon self and produces self-pity, it becomes a reprehensible and a carnal thing. The principal
of our boarding school in India called a teacher's meeting
in his bungalow. He placed sufficient chairs for all in the

living room. One lady teacher sat in a chair near the piano and being ill at ease fidgeted until the chair walked right over against the piano, where its finish was in danger of being scratched. The principal saw what was happening but managed to close the meeting without saying anything. Two weeks later he held another meeting, but he took particular pains to see that the chair was a good three feet away from the piano. But the same lady teacher came and sat in the same chair and fidgeted in the same way until the chair again walked up to the piano. This was too much. So the principal requested her very kindly to move her chair enough so that it would not scratch the piano. She moved the chair, and then sat hurt and silent through the rest of the meeting. For the next couple of days she kept out of sight. On the third day the principal met her on the walk, where she requested a letter of recommendation to another school because she felt unworthy to teach in his school since spoiling his piano. That seems pretty childish of course. But the incident tends to highlight this matter of sensitiveness. Thank God there is a happy sequel to the story. This girl later experienced the fullness of the Spirit and her life now is very different.

Now it is not the will of God that sensitiveness should be "eradicated." But it must be cleansed of its self-centeredness and set free to express the glory of God. Where this capacity has been carnal and has constituted a real problem in one's life, the cleansing of the self-centeredness out of the sensitiveness often constitutes a very remarkable deliverance.

I know another Spirit-filled Indian brother who is blessed with an unusual capacity for being sensitive to the suffering of others. It drives him to endless labors and he has a passion for souls which is rare. But the devil always attacks us on the points of our greatest strength, and this brother frequently has terrific spiritual battles over feeling sorry for himself. Why should he give so much of himself for others when other preachers who get more money give so little of themselves and suffer so little inconvenience? How easily these qualities given to us as instruments for the service of God may be twisted into instruments for self, and how easily can the devil create situations where the legitimate use of an instrument becomes the occasion of the withdrawal of self from its hidden place in God and of its setting up in independence again.

This may be clearer from a study of envy. No one will suggest that envy has a legitimate side but that is because our English word is limited to only the bad side of a two-fold experience. In I Corinthians 13:4 we are told that love "envieth not." But actually the Greek word is *dzeloi*, meaning excitement of mind, ardor, fervor of spirit. This is capable of being exercised in both a good and a bad way. In the good way it is zeal for, ardor in embracing, pursuing or defending a good thing. "The *zeal* of thine house hath eaten me up" (John 2:17) is a case in point. The Corinthians responded to Paul's exhortations with "what clearing of yourselves, yea, what indignation, yea, what fear, yea, what vehement desire, yea, what *zeal*, yea, what revenge! In all things ye have approved yourselves to be clear in this matter" (II Cor. 7:11). Yet on the other hand this quality may be exercised in an evil way. In this evil way it is envy, contentious rivalry, jealousy (as in Rom. 13:13, "Let us walk . . . not in strife and *envying*").

On the surface, zeal and envy seem to have little in common, but an illustration will make plain their relationship. Suppose some election is to take place in your church — perhaps it is for Sunday School Superintendent. Two names are before the people and yours is one. You like Sunday School work. In fact, you feel very responsible toward it and can give yourself to the work with zeal. You have abilities which will enable you to do the job creditably and to the glory of God. The other name represents a good man, but candidly you suspect he has less love for this work than you have, and not quite the same ability. The election takes place. The people are not always as wise as they ought to be. The other man is elected! You protest to your friends

that this is much the better thing and you congratulate the
new Superintendent and tell him you will pray for him.
But down in your heart of hearts you wonder. *Was* it
God's will? How zealous you had been to serve in this
way. Then you begin to watch your brother carefully. It
is your zeal for the Lord's work. You want him to make
good, you tell yourself. He makes some blunders. Then
some carelessness is in evidence. How you wish you could
help. You do not want to see the Sunday School suffer.
Your zeal is intense. Then more blunders. You try to forget. But it keeps bothering you. You just can't forget.
And to make a long story short, you wake up one day to
the fact that you have a full-blown case of envy on your
hands.

Now just when does one cross the line between zeal and
envy? How can one tell when he crosses or is in danger
of crossing? And what happens to his sanctification if he
should cross? These are important questions which must
be answered after we look at additional illustrations.

The tongue seems to be the chief problem of some folk,
and a real problem to us all. Now obviously there is no
"eradication" of the tongue. But it is equally obvious that
one cannot let it run without control, even in the life of
holiness.

I was once attending a convention for the deepening of
spiritual life in India. A friend of mine in that Mission
had a very exacting spirit. He was virtually always right
in what he said, but the manner he used had left a long
train of heartache and wounded spirits. He had sought
deliverance, claimed victory, and there had been great improvement. Then on the opening day of the convention
he spoke to an Indian brother about that brother's conduct.
Again he was right, but again his manner set off tempers
and the resulting explosion threatened to blow the convention right off the calendar. The missionary went into se-
clusion. The next morning I found him in his tent packing
his suitcase, in the depths of discouragement. It was no use.

He had failed again, he was unworthy as a missionary, and he intended to go home. After a little talk and prayer he entered the next meeting with a new victory. There he rose before his Indian brethren, humbly apologized, and then said an interesting thing. "If my trouble were something like liquor or tobacco, it would be easy to deal with. I could simply throw them away and be done with them. But my problem is my tongue. I know that I cannot cut it out to the glory of God. I have committed my all afresh, including my tongue, to God, trusting that the Holy Spirit will cleanse and help me to use it to His glory."

There are two common errors with regard to the use of the tongue. The first is to suppose that we are helpless in the hands of our sinful nature, that an offensive tongue is something about which God's grace does nothing in this life, and that we must control it as best we may, but with little hope of acquiring anything better than our nature provides. The other error is to suppose that the eradication of the carnal nature leaves the tongue so cleansed as to need no discipline. The truth is that the cleansing of the heart — the elimination of our willful enmity against God — does provide a cleansing within every part of our equipment, including our tongues, and makes every part ready to speak to God's glory. The tongue is then ready for intense discipline, as James faithfully testifies. God does something for us. He cleanses us and gives us power to do something for ourselves. There is much left for us to do. Cleansing and discipline are two watchwords, two apparent contradictories, which must be caught up in a living paradox if we want God's best. Then we can say that He does for us something which we could never do for ourselves. No amount of discipline would ever control the tongue if it were still expressing the abundance of a heart in which there was enmity against God. While God does something for us which we could not do *by* our disciplining, yet He does it in order to make it possible *for* us to discipline our lives to His glory.

Every once in a while we hear someone say, "Well, I just told him off — you know I'm made that way — I just have to say what comes to my mind!" There is no doubt that many people do say what comes to their mind, but it is a lame defense to say that they *have* to. What we all have to do is to *control* sternly our tongues, and we cannot hope to get on well with this unless we submit our hearts to the cleansing which leaves our selves hid with Christ in God.

It is entirely consistent with our hidden place in God that we should still be subject to much of human infirmity. We shall often, with the best of intentions and with much of discipline, give a word of offense. The Spirit-filled heart is not evidenced by attaining a state of grace in which we never are caught off guard and say a wounding word, but rather by the quickness and fullness with which we find ourselves ready to make amends when it comes to our consciousness that offense has been taken. Here it is not enough that we should feel clear in our intentions when we speak. "If thy brother *have ought against thee* . . . go to him. . . ." A disposition to apologize, to come quickly to terms, to heal a wound, to satisfy an offended brother: this *disposition* is the test for holiness, not the elimination of every offending word.

Jesus was before the high priest when an officer struck Him with the palm of his hand. Jesus replied: "If I have spoken evil, bear witness of the evil: but if well, why smitest thou me?" (John 18:23). If you will ponder this answer for an hour you can think of no possible improvement. Under the greatest provocation, still Jesus gives an absolutely perfect answer.

At a later date, the Apostle Paul found himself in an identical situation (Acts 23:1-5). When the high priest's servant smote him on the mouth, Paul said, "God shall smite thee, thou whited wall: for sittest thou to judge me after the law, and commandest me to be smitten contrary to the law?"

Now this is something else. One does not have to think

long to be able to improve on this speech. Not but that it was mostly true. Perhaps it was all true — even to the "whited wall" if that phrase were properly interpreted. But the spirit of it is not the spirit of Christ's remark. Calling names, using epithets, throwing labels at folk is not of the Spirit of Christ. It is true that Jesus once called the Pharisees "serpents," and a "generation of vipers" (Matt. 23:33). But as in the case of the reference to the Syro-phenician woman as a "dog," we need to understand the connotation of "serpent" in His day. Furthermore, whereas our name-calling is usually a sudden burst of temper, this word of Jesus comes as a climax to a long denunciation of the hypocrisy of the Pharisees, the whole tenor of which, while exceedingly penetrating, is yet so restrained that one does not feel the flash of self in His words. Our indignation is rarely as righteous. No matter how true or right may have been Paul's words, the total impression they gave to the hearers was that he was reviling the high priest.

Now what about Paul? Was he Spirit-filled? Was he fully surrendered? Was he hid with Christ in God?

We must make clear that all these questions concern disposition rather than outward or absolute perfection. There is proof that Paul was surrendered, that he was Spirit-filled. But the proof lies not in any experience which would make his answers, his words, the use of his tongue as perfect as those of Jesus. Rather the proof lies in the *disposition* which he manifested as soon as his error was revealed. Instantly, upon the rebuke of the bystanders, Paul came through with an apology. That indicated more truly the real heart of the man. And so it will with us. Caught off guard, a word is spoken, an attitude taken or a spirit shown for which we receive the Spirit's rebuke. If, in that situation, we allow self to re-affirm its independent stand, if we slip out of our hidden place in God, if a bit of enmity against God creeps back in, that will be manifest by an unwillingness to heed the check of the Spirit and a stubborn decision to go right on. Usually there is something more cutting still ready to be said, and one says it. But if there is love for Christ above all else and a desire to be altogether His, that disposition will show itself, even in so stern and tempestuous a nature as Paul's, with complete readiness to apologize and make right the incident. Note also that Paul's action was instant — he did not wait for three or four days to cool off and then come around and merely try to act pleasant as though nothing had ever happened! The Spirit-filled heart does not hold grudges.

We are far from exhausting the phases of human nature which must be cleansed and regulated to the glory of God in the sanctified life. But before proceeding to further illustrations we must give answer to the questions we have been holding over until now. How can we know when we have crossed the line from legitimate hunger to gluttony, from sensitiveness about the condition of others to self-pity, from zeal to envy, and from holy to unholy speech?

The answer is simple. No man can tell me when I cross the line, nor can I tell another when he crosses his line. Nor is there any set of rules which will help either of us. *We are shut up to the guidance of the Holy Spirit.* It is a living way and nothing short of the Living Spirit of God dwelling within us can solve our problem. *But He does guide us!* There is never a time when we are in danger of crossing one of these lines but that He faithfully speaks! Yet never thunderously — only with a still small voice. We can always hear — *if we listen!*

I have spoken of "crossing the line." Actually there is an area between that which is clearly and wholly for the glory of God and that which is clearly and wholly for the glory of the isolated self — a sort of twilight zone. As one enters it, the Spirit begins to whisper words of caution. These grow more intense as we approach the line. Crossing, there is a feeling of condemnation and guilt which intensifies the further we go. It is not simple, partly because of our dullness of hearing and perception, and partly because of the complex nature of the situation — the intertwining of the legitimate with the sinful in that shaded area. It is something like sunset. On shipboard I have watched the sun set into the sea in a cloudless sky. The horizon is a sharp line and there is not an instant's doubt when the sun has gone. But often sunset is complicated by the presence of clouds and an irregular horizon or skyline. Sometimes we are aware, especially on cloudy and drizzly days, only of a gradual loss of light when twilight turns to dark. So too in Christian living. It is impossible to reduce the matter to simple rules or to define exactly the line in all cases. We are shut up to the voice of the Spirit as our only guide.

And suppose we fail. Suppose we cross the line and do the thing the Holy Spirit rebuked. What then is our condition and what can we do about it?

First of all, let us recognize our condition as sinful. It must not be covered up by reference to the wonder of our original crisis experience of surrender and cleansing or sanctification. Too many have thus accumulated a lot of unforgiven sin by assuming that since they had such a glorious experience back there, and carnality was eradicated, that surely nothing now can be wrong. Whatever eradication means — or crucifixion, or putting to death the old man — it is not a chunk of something *material* that is done away. Rather, it is a wrong *relationship* between us and God that is destroyed. But just because it is a relationship, an immaterial rather than a material something, it can as quickly be reinstated as destroyed. The cure, then, is fresh repentance and forgiveness and cleansing as we put the relationship right again. And happy is the one who has learned to make this adjustment instantly and quickly.

3

The Spirit-Controlled Life

Pride is something reprehensible in its self-centered form, and yet it has a counterpart which is glorifying to God. What we call self-respect may be a thing which God can bless. God takes no particular pleasure in our looking sloppy — even when the styles are that way — in our failing through carelessness, in our being satisfied with the bottom of the ladder. Yet it is perfectly obvious that our dress and our ambitions may be, and very often are, clear evidences of pride.

We Quakers once tried to curb pride in the hearts of our members by legislating the precise length of skirts and sleeves and the exact style and cut of coats and dresses. Buttons were sinful for they were decorative rather than merely useful. Grey was the standard color. Men could not wear neckties and their coats could not have lapels, — for these, too, were merely decorative. Collars were square and coats were fastened together by invisible and, therefore, non-decorative hooks and eyes. The minutes of business meetings of that period were full of rules and regulations and of disciplinary action taken against offenders.

Principles of modesty and simplicity are clearly set forth in Scripture. But there still remains the problem of applying these and reducing the general principle to the specific instance. There are two false methods of handling this

situation. One is to forget it all on the assumption that
clothes have nothing to do with the Gospel. The other is
to pass regulations prescribing a uniform, with strict meas-
ures covering every detail of one's outfit. These are the
ways of death. We must find a living way.

How then can we tell when we have crossed the line from
a legitimate, God-honoring self-respect to a pride which is
carnal and selfish? How can we know which clothes are
consistent with self-respect and which ones minister to pride?
It should be noted that merely being colorless or ugly does
not eliminate pride. Some folks are proud of their ugliness.
It is so distinctive! And John Wesley wrote a sermon on
the subject of dress in which he said that he hoped some
day to see a Methodist congregation as plainly clad as
Quakers, but mind you, he said, that there be no "Quaker
linen."[1] The reference is to the practice of wealthy Quakers who went to Paris to find materials of the prescribed
shade of grey which would be sufficiently elegant to show
their wealthy station in life.

A wild-fire young Indian evangelist came into our church
once and suddenly ordered everyone present to take off their
shoes and put them outside the door — not only to conform
with Indian custom but to observe some obscure Old Testament passage. No one moved. A missionary protested that
we were not living in the Old Testament. But the young
fellow was insistent that only pride made people wear their
shoes in the church. I found the confused congregation
looking in my direction, so I spoke. I told the brother I
hoped I was not proud of my shoes, and to prove it I would
put them outside the door — which I promptly did. Then
I proceeded to stand in my socks and give a message on the
subtlety of pride, which may be just as evident in a minister
in his supposed power to lord it over a congregation as in
anyone's dress.

Indeed this is important, for there is a legitimate field
for ambition which may be used for the glory of God. Min-

1. John Wesley, *Sermons on Several Occasions,* "On Dress," pp. 26, 27.

isters and servants of God are by no means exempt from ambitions, particularly the ambition to be at their best in the service of the Lord. Every preacher wants to preach a good sermon. But it is one of the subtlest fields of the devil's work to pull a man across the line from wanting to preach a good sermon for God's glory to the point where his inner satisfaction becomes pride. Can he keep a sense that it was all the gift of God or does he begin to "recognize" his own considerable ability? Every Spirit-filled heart may be encouraged by words of appreciation. But when does this become a love of flattery? Does that situation just take care of itself when one is Spirit-filled? Decidedly not! The sanctified life is an intensely disciplined life or it soon ceases to be sanctified. And one occasion that calls for drastic discipline is when the preacher meets his admiring parishioners at the door after he has done tolerably well.

One of my best missionary friends in India, now retired, tells of a time when as a student he was sent out to be the evangelist for a revival meeting. Another student was sent along as song leader. After a few days he noticed that more people came forward to shake hands with the song leader than with the preacher. In another day or so he knew that he had to do something about this or lose victory. So he went to the song leader and arranged to have him preach the next night, and by this self-abasement he won the victory. His action was part of that discipline of the cleansed human nature which is necessary to keep it from reverting to carnal nature. Every preacher needs something better than a book of rules to show him through the maze of temptations which are directed at him in particular to push his legitimate ambitions for the advancement of the kingdom across the line into the field of personal pride. In fear and trembling he needs to hang across his conscience like a banner of fire that word of the Lord from ancient times: "His glory He will not share with another."

To exercise authority while recognizing that all authority is derived from above is a most exacting spiritual test.

Someone said that supervision ought to be 90 per cent "vi-sion" and not more than 10 per cent "super." Obviously nothing short of the living presence of the Holy Spirit whispering His little checks will save us from re-infecting our holy self-respect with carnal pride. As Oswald Chambers well said: "One of the outstanding miracles of God's grace is to make us able to take any kind of leadership at all with-out losing spiritual power."[2]

Another most troublesome item of human nature is the temper. No part of our equipment is more necessary, and no part more easily prostituted to selfishness. There is a common misconception that temper is eradicated by sancti-fication, or should be. Awful confusion attends this error, which results either in hypocrisy or loss of confidence. Temper is no more eradicated than is the self. But it must be cleansed and, along with the self, be hid with Christ in God. Temper is part of God's creation. Without it we would be worthless. It is simply a phase of the emotional life. If we had no temper we would placidly stand in the path of an oncoming car, unmoved by the sound of the horn and unable to escape death. Temper enables us to react to wrong situations in ways which tend to change and redeem those situations. This is particularly true where the wrong is moral in character. God wants us to feel stirred and stirred deeply by the sight of evil. Spineless Christianity, temperless in the face of grave wrongs, is not of God. We sometimes forget that one of the commands of Scripture is, "Be ye angry" (Eph. 4:26). But with the com-mand goes instantly the recognition that in actual practice it is more difficult to keep the temper hid with Christ in God than any other part of our equipment. This is be-cause the temper along with our whole emotional life is re-flexive in character and is controlled by the involuntary autonomic nervous system.

Psychologists have noted that a baby is born with innate responses such as fear of a loud noise near the head and

2. Oswald Chambers, *The Message of Invincible Consolation*, p. 19.

anger at having its movements restrained. As life goes on, these elemental emotions become conditioned by ever more complex situations. And into the complexity comes, as a further complicating factor, the bias of the carnal mind. Since emotional reactions are involuntary, they form an excellent mirror of the heart. If the heart is impure it will be revealed in flashes of selfish temper. After cleansing, the temper will still work involuntarily, but it should reflect the new and holy condition of the heart. Furthermore, those feelings which rise involuntarily must be subjected to rigid discipline.

"Be ye angry, and sin not." To this is then added good practical advice for the disciplining of righteous anger so as to keep it from being the instrument of the return of that mind which is enmity against God: "Let not the sun go down upon your wrath." It is as though one said, Take off this righteous anger before you go to bed at night, and hang it up like a coat. The next morning scrutinize it carefully and very prayerfully before putting it on again, to see whether it is really righteous and worth taking up again.

We must recognize clearly the distinction between emotional impulses which are controlled by the autonomic nervous system and which arise quite involuntarily, and emotional states which are permitted to continue voluntarily. There are great individual differences in the speed and strength of involuntary impulses. Indeed, we call some people "impulsive," meaning that by nature they react more suddenly and violently than others to situations.

There is a sense in which these strong sudden feelings do indicate the inner nature. Selfishness may thus be revealed. But it does not necessarily follow that the slow and steady person is unselfish because he does not suddenly show temper. What is more important is to look at the area of emotional states which we voluntarily permit or condone. For instance, on the good side, the joy of the Lord as our strength is an emotional attitude deliberately maintained by a choice independent of circumstances. On the bad side are feelings of resentment, bitterness or anger which are tolerated, nursed and perpetuated over a period of time.

Not all of the wrong situations which stir us deeply are great moral issues. Take the matter of orderliness. Disorderliness in the home, or in business, or in the work of the Lord bothers an orderly mind. God intended it to be so. He Himself is a God of order. He wants us to feel strongly about disorderliness, else we would never do anything about it. But if we are blessed with a sense of order, we shall have to exercise patience with those who are not, while they must strive to be orderly just because God is orderly. Our problem arises in that it is so easy in this field for our sense of the wrongness in a disorderly situation to arise not from the fact of God's orderliness but from a personal and selfish frustration or inconvenience. The children are having a romp around the house. It is raining, so they cannot play outside. We want to read or write or listen to the radio. By what scale can we determine whether our concern for quiet is for the children's good and the glory of God or merely for our own personal comfort?

The answer to this question, along with those raised above, is simply a deep sensitiveness to the voice of the Holy Spirit, which cautions us as to the impure character of the temper we are about to indulge. It should be clear that there is a legitimate temper and that God is not pleased with disorder, but that one easily crosses a line where this legitimate temper becomes an instrument of self in a selfish state.

In Paul's Hymn to Love he states that "love is not easily provoked" (I Cor. 13:5). The word translated "provoked" is, like all of the terms used in this passage to define the characteristics of love, usable in two senses, a good and a bad. The word here is *paroxunetai*, which comes over into English as *paroxysm*. Literally it means *to make sharp*. To illustrate its two senses we may see two incidents in Paul's life. In Athens he walked the streets, saw the innumerable idols, and "his spirit was stirred in him" (Acts 17:16). In other words, he had a paroxysm. The idolatry around him made sharp his sense of wrong. This sense obviously was consistent with divine love. But there was another time when the contention grew so sharp (paroxysm) between Paul and Barnabas that they separated. Probably this paroxysm was of the sort which Paul later conceded was not of love. Both incidents show Paul's temper stirred, the one time righteously, the other of doubtful indignation. Yet we cannot judge finally, and that is true of all this line-crossing which I have tried to set forth. We cannot finally judge another as to when the good becomes the evil. We can only say, If I were in that case, I should be convicted. The only righteous judge is Christ Himself. Thank God, for He is entirely faithful. And He is prepared to speak, passing judgment on every involuntary flash of temper, if we discipline ourselves to listen.

To go much further would be wearisome. But it should be clear that any part of our human nature can be looked at in the same way. Reason itself may be useful to save us from error — or it may stoop to rationalizing, where our selfish wishes are made respectable to ourselves. Imagination is valuable for formulating plans for the furtherance of the kingdom, for producing useful inventions and for solving difficult problems — or it may be prostituted to the level of idle day dreaming which feeds our vanity, picturing us in situations which get us much applause for passing for far more than we are worth, or causing us to imagine meanings and motives in the actions of others which are not there.

I started with the urge to hunger. All our urges can be treated likewise. At times there crops up in circles stressing the deeper life in the Spirit a misconception that sex is wrong, carnal, and selfish. Some even think it ought to be eradicated. A great need in our day is to set forth an adequate message on the sanctification of sex. There seems to be a supposition that all the attendant pleasures of the sexual life are vaguely but somehow carnal. This reminds

one of the Stoic eating fish. What we need to see is that
God created the pleasures of eating and sex just as surely as
He created the urges themselves, and that their enjoyment
can be sanctified to His glory. Quite obviously these may
likewise be made ends in themselves and prostituted to the
low level of selfishness and sin. Sex outside wedlock is of
course an instance of this. No rationalizing can make it
right. It is sin.

But our borderline difficulties lie on a different plane. It
is where sexual attraction works in those mild, preliminary
ways which are subtle. Here again, the attraction is a God-
given thing. The biological fact that male and female at-
tract one another like the negative and positive poles of
magnets is entirely holy. Without that attraction there
would of course be no love, courtship or marriage. Nor
can we suppose that either sanctification *or marriage* removes it. This is not eradicated. But when cleansed and
hid with Christ in God, it can be effectively disciplined.
The sanctified Apostle said, "I maul and master my body"
(I Cor. 9:29, Moffatt). Before marriage this impulse in
the sanctified will be disciplined so as to save them from
improper liberties in courtship and from giving their affec-
tions to partners outside the Lord.

It is a mistake, of course, to suppose that this attraction
in itself is the sufficient ground for choice of a life partner.
Just because two young people feel they love each other is
no adequate reason for marriage. Such pathetic things happen when a young person who has claimed to be a Christian
accepts a partner who is not, and justifies it with the inadequate reason that they love each other! This attraction is
to be disciplined even to denial, when it cannot be satisfied
in the Lord.

It is also a mistake to suppose that this attraction operates
only between two people entirely meant for each other by
God. Sexual attraction works pretty generally as a biological
fact, and because this is true married couples who have
plighted their troth must exercise discipline as well as the

unmarried. In our modern pagan civilization these biological urges have been accepted as masters, and our modern pagans expect neither to give nor receive faithfulness for any length of time. When the newness wears off there is an increasing number of new attractions. This is a fact. Pagans yield to it. Christians discipline themselves in the Lord.

Now there are certain simple features of this attraction which are constantly at work. Indian society pretty well admits no middle ground between initial attraction and sexual consummation. That is why their society permits no free mingling of the sexes, no courtship, and in its extreme forms puts its women behind a curtain or in a *burkha.* The theory is that what a man cannot see he will not desire. Western civilization looks upon the matter differently. In India there is no thought of inner controls — they must all be external. No man is trusted; rather he is restricted. But Western civilization owes a great debt to Christ for the idea of inner control — that a man in Christ may be trusted even in the dark, and that impulses may be felt — even enjoyed — under a discipline which restrains and controls them. We do not feel it necessary to hang a veil over a pretty woman's face in order to keep men from being tempted to immorality. We assume that there is a place where a man in Christ may see, admire, and feel pleasure in such a face, having the doors of his mind closed to further satisfactions of the sexual attraction which lies implicit in the experience.

From the pretty face it is a short step to notice the beautiful form. To women this same element of sexual attraction is present but in altered form. A dashing personality may be just as devastating to a woman as a beautiful form to a man. Women may be in more danger because personality is so much more subtle than physical form. Now the important fact to bear in mind is that this attraction in itself is not sin; it is not carnal; it is definitely present in the Spirit-filled. But while it is a thing of real beauty which puts zest in life without jeopardizing marital faithfulness or real holiness, yet sexual attraction is as dangerous as it is subtle, and it calls for rigid discipline.

The lustful look condemned by Jesus is not necessarily so. The fact of attraction, appreciation and pleasure regarding a woman's beauty is not sin or carnal in itself. But it is extremely easy to cross the line where this legitimate exercise of God-given impulse becomes an occasion for self to slip out into independence again, and for the look to become carnal. Probably when one becomes aware of his look taking on aspects of improper desire he is crossing over and must exercise discipline. But this question of crossing the line, in this as in so many other areas which we have set forth, leaves us utterly dependent upon the still small voice of the Holy Spirit for its answer.

What is said here applies not only to men. Women, too, have their moments of great attraction to men for reasons which they could scarcely explain. Some have felt this to be a carnal surge within them. If there has been no full surrender maintained to that moment, this might be so. But even in the Spirit-filled heart these moments of attraction, of extreme awareness of the presence of a well-liked man or of a specially attractive woman, may mean no more than the presence of this God-created urge, may indicate no disloyalty either to one's spouse or to Christ, and may be in keeping with the general enjoyment of free commingling of the sexes allowed in our civilization and indeed in the Christian church of all time and everywhere.

Yet it is obvious that the devil's way into the hearts of many men and women is to begin to pull on this natural and legitimate element and to cause momentary enjoyment to grow into a pleasure demanding more and more satisfaction. If the heart is truly pure, there will be an instant willingness to apply discipline, to have done with the pleasure, putting it from one's self when the realization comes that it is becoming dangerous or unholy. But the very pleasure of free commingling will be used by the enemy to set up an insistent clamor for more and more satisfaction, and if the self yields to this clamor and comes out of its hidden, surrendered place in God, it will become insistent on having a little more pleasure instead of obeying the checks, and thus it gives way to a carnal, selfish state again.

It must be clear by now that the sanctified life is basically life lived utterly under the control, moment by moment, of the Holy Spirit. How can we know when we have crossed the line from legitimate hunger to gluttony, from holy sensitiveness or anger to that which is carnal, from zeal to envy, from holy to unholy speech, from self-respect to pride, from pleasure in beauty to the lustful look, and from the holy to the unholy use of sex?

The first element in the answer is that none of us can tell each other when he has crossed the line. My friend's conversation about a third friend may impress me as being more of envy than of zeal, but I cannot possibly know just what are his inner light and motives. Nor can I know just when, *for him,* the line has been crossed. I may observe that his conduct in this particular is a lesson to me and that I could not under similar circumstances do the same thing without being convicted. Whether it would actually register in that way in my consciousness if I were actually in the same circumstances, is another question, but it ought to be so. *Obviously, I must not judge my brother.* I may judge myself severely the next time I am caught in similar circumstances, but I cannot know what light has come to my brother.

An infinite amount of trouble and misunderstanding among Christians arises out of this persistent temptation to judge others, imputing motives which we have no right to impute. It is true that we are to exercise righteous judgment and that the power to weigh evidence and choose the good and reject the bad, the critical faculty, is a part of the equipment God has given us. With this, evil may be cut off from the church. But here is one more case where a legitimate God-given quality can become the agent of self. What is there which is so ready to Satan's hand with which to pull at the vanity of our minds as the pride of our opinions and judgments?

It has not yet dawned in the minds of many Christians that the pride of opinion is just as damning and must be dealt with just as decisively as any other sin. Of course the answer always is, "But I am right!" That is the way we always feel about our judgments. It is in the very nature of judgment that it should carry with it an emotional tone which we call conviction or certainty. But suppose two sanctified people hold opposite judgments. Each feels the other is wrong. Actually both are wrong if there is not a disposition to yield! So I must stop passing judgment on whether my brother is sanctified when he wears things I cannot wear without pride, or speaks more explosively than I would let myself under provocation, or seems too sensitive about the criticisms I have given for his good. I just do not know whether he has crossed his line in these matters or not, and he is not judged before God by my line.

But I have a line. *And I know when I cross it!* God sees to that! Life in the Spirit does not operate by sheer momentum of inertia, nor by rules and regulations, nor yet again by the judgments of men, good and helpful though these may be by times. The sanctified life is *life!* And it can only be lived in the Holy Spirit. He it is who, when put in full control of our hearts, stands ready to whisper whenever we approach the line. His checks and promptings are absolutely faithful. He will always whisper — and we shall hear if we listen. The sad part is that we so often fail to listen. One missionary, who had precipitated an ugly situation by a certain speech, told me, when I asked whether he really felt led to make that speech: "No. I felt I must say it quickly for fear I would be checked before I got it said." That was more honest than most of us care to be, but how often that has been our experience.

The Holy Spirit's guidance, then, is our only answer. Most folk want a sanctification that will work itself. Human nature is essentially lazy. People want spectacular experi-

ences which will give them in an instant a sanctification like
a chunk of something all wrapped up and labeled and ready
to be shipped through to glory without further attention.
Not so, however, for Christ offers *life*. Many have been at-
tracted to the doctrine of "eradication" in the hope of having
all their problems and particularly the need for effort and
discipline eradicated from their lives. This is not "scriptural
holiness." On the other hand, to try to discipline one's
life without first having the pattern of life which revolved
around self as a center eradicated by a surrender which brings
cleansing and the hiding of the self with Christ in God, is
futile and doomed to defeat. Only the living of a life
disciplined by the guidance and control of the Holy Spirit
brings knowledge of the path of continual victory.

Sanctification is both a crisis and a process. Neither is
possible without the other. It should be clear by now how
easy it would be to lose what one received in the crisis — to
leave one's hidden place with Christ in God and slip back
to the easy old self-life again. There is no way to victory
except a walk of carefulness under the constant guidance
and in instant obedience to the Holy Spirit. Whether this
seems hard or not, depends largely on whether we have made
the great committal or not. If we love Jesus Christ as we
ought to love Him, with all there is of us and without reser-
vation, then this will seem not arduous but a glorious, victorious life of love and service for Him. To the unsurrendered it will seem irksome and dreary indeed.

4

The Guidance of the Spirit

Every high spiritual privilege carries with it immense peril. The greater the privilege the greater the peril. Divine guidance is a precious privilege fraught with peculiar peril. Yet we dare not neglect it, for "as many as are led by the Spirit of God, they are the sons of God" (Rom. 8:14).

As a boy trying to be a Christian, I was greatly puzzled by the testimonies of adult Christians who would say that God had spoken to them and told them to do thus and so. I listened intently but no voice broke on my ears. As a Quaker boy my heritage included the remarkable stories of people who in spectacular ways received direction from God. There were those two women who in the beginnings of Quakerism felt impressed of the Spirit to carry a Gospel message in person to the Sultan of Turkey. It was difficult for anyone to see the Sultan in those days and for two single women to make the journey alone was quite unthinkable. But God told them to go. They were not only given audience but their message was kindly received. The Sultan, realizing the dangers attendant upon single women traveling through Turkey, offered them an armed guard from the capital to the border. This they refused, saying that they felt safer in God's keeping than in that of soldiers.

Then there was Stephen Grellet, French nobleman who missed the guillotine, escaped to America and became a leading Quaker preacher. Amid his arduous travels in America he was once led of the Spirit to go and preach in a certain logging camp. Although he found the camp deserted he was so sure of his leadings that he stood up and preached in an empty dining hall. Years later in London a man approached Grellet, reminded him of the incident, said that he was the cook of the camp and the only man around that day. Seeing a preacher come, he hid, and listened outside the window. He was so impressed by the sermon, given without an audience, that, although at the time remaining concealed, he was convicted and converted, and from then on did a large Christian service.[1]

Again, there were the remarkable and often discomfiting insights into individual spiritual needs by the late Amos Kenworthy. And in my own Yearly Meeting there was Esther Butler, who fifty years ago founded our Mission in China. When called of God to that pioneer work, she saw a crowded Chinese street in a vision, the faces and places of which she later clearly recognized upon arrival in Nanking.[2]

How could I get God to speak to me like that? Many young friends were in those days claiming calls of God to service in foreign lands. I wanted to go desperately, but for the life of me I could not honestly say that I had any experience which I could label a call from God. I interviewed preachers, missionaries, and church officials, but mostly I got only the instruction to be sure to obey when the will of God was revealed. I had settled that long before. What I needed now was instruction as to how to hear the voice of God. One good pastor comforted me somewhat by relating an incident. Some new convert asked Amos Kenworthy how it was that Christ had said, "My sheep know my voice," yet he couldn't hear Christ's voice. The aged saint replied, "Yes, it is true that His sheep know His voice but it is also true that the lambs have to learn it." That

1. William Wistar Comfort, *Stephen Grellett,* pp. 42, 43.
2. Walter R. Williams, *Ohio Friends in the Land of Sinim,* p. 21.

helped some. But if only I could know how to begin to learn, how happy I would be.

Later I found two very helpful books, Upham's *Inward Divine Guidance* and Knapp's *Impressions*. Then came simple little experiences in which I applied the tests as best I could. Most of my earliest experiences were in the form of guidance to speak to boyhood companions about becoming Christians. I found in almost every case where I was truly led that the person was prepared by the Spirit to receive my invitation. It worried me a bit that I could not describe that guidance to myself in any more substantial terms than that when my fear reached a certain stage of nervous tension, then I knew it was time to go and speak to the one on my heart. If it was not of God, the fear subsided. Later I recognized that the voice of God did not consist of an experience of being scared but rather in the growth of an inner conviction. In those days that particular conviction carried an emotional tone of fright for me, but I gradually came to realize that it was the sense of conviction that counted rather than any emotion, pleasant or unpleasant, with which it might be associated.

About that time I heard another helpful thing from some preacher. He said that the devil moves people on sudden impulse but that God always gives us time for consideration, the application of tests, and the growth of conviction. He went so far as to say that whenever we were seized with a sudden impulse to do something odd and to do it quickly, we could be practically sure that the impression had come from the devil. In the main this has proved true in my later experience. God is love; He does not give us guidance as a form of punishment but rather as a loving expression of His interest in the affairs of our lives. He is therefore patient, and glad to have us assured of His will before we act. God does speak when we listen and it works out in experience. It is a glorious privilege. We must have done with fear — even fear of making mistakes — if we would learn to know the voice of God. In a quiet time it is possible to receive impulses from Satan or merely from one's own desires, as well as from God. One will need to apply some simple tests by which to screen these impulses.

First, *Is the impression Scriptural?* God never violates His written Word. The Holy Spirit can always be depended upon to be consistent. Any impression which is not consistent with the Scriptures did not originate with Him. One of the most profound reasons why a Christian should be a constant and consistent student of the Word is that thereby he comes better to know the mind of Christ. The first, and primary, test must be constantly applied. Word and Spirit go together.

Second, *Is it right?* God never requires immoral acts. I knew a married man who approached a single lady and asked for her hand in marriage, saying that the Lord had revealed this as His will. Evidently the wires were crossed. So were they when the mother of several small children felt that she should leave her family and go alone to Africa as a missionary.

Third, *Is it providential?* Do circumstances, all of which we may believe are either in the active or the permissive will of God, converge to open the doors for the accomplishment of the object about which we have been impressed? If God is calling, He will always open the doors — we need not force them.

Fourth, *Is it corroborated by trusted and Spirit-led friends?* This is a necessary check against unbridled individualism. It is conceivable that the individual may be right in standing against a group of Christians, but it is most dangerous. I think there is a better way. The late Amos Kenworthy, who is known for his instant revelation and spiritual insight, was a man whom most folk regarded as next to infallible. Nevertheless, I am told that he faithfully adhered to the Quaker principle of submitting his concerns to the fellowship of the elders and overseers of the meeting, and went on his errands of ministry only when they united with him.

Usually they endorsed his concern, granting, according to the custom of Friends, a written "minute" expressing their unity with him in this service. This credential he was careful to carry with him in the discharge of his concern. But occasionally the "Select Meeting" did not concur with his guidance. It was then that he left the responsibility for that service with the fellowship of the group and submitted to their judgment. This to me is the deepest proof that he was led of God. The fellowship is of extreme importance — granted of course that it is a true fellowship in the Spirit.

Finally, *Does the impression become an ever more weighty conviction?* For me this has been the heart of guidance. Many an idea has seized me with great enthusiasm. Then to my surprise it faded out over a short period of time. But the voice of God is in a conviction which grows with the passing of time and becomes inescapable and compelling.

I must hasten to guard against two wrong impressions which I may have given. First, it must not be assumed that knowing God's will for life service is only for preachers and missionaries. I thank God for a host of young Christians in business and professional life who are just as sure of God's will for their lives as any preacher could be for his. Secondly, it must not be supposed that divine guidance is only for great crisis decisions of life. The Holy Spirit is interested in the detailed conduct of our daily lives to the end that they should be Christlike. Much He leaves to the realm of our sanctified judgment. But there is possible to us an ever deepening and conscious dependence upon Him for direction in the small matters. Neither must it be supposed from my extended discussion of the tests of guidance that obtaining the mind of the Lord must always be a lengthy and labored process. Rather, it is true that with experience one can soon discover that same quality of conviction that *is* guidance attaching itself to impressions concerning small details of the daily program during the quiet time. Weightier matters about which there is some uncertainty may well be held over for another day or more extended periods of time to allow for the crystallization or the fading of the conviction as the case may be.

Life is terribly inadequate unless caught up into the vital, adventurous realm of daily divine guidance where the Holy Spirit controls, not in some vague deistic sense, but in an intimate relationship where our losing ourselves in Him is so real that He becomes our intelligence, our heart, our will, our very life. In this intimate relationship the discipline of the early morning quiet time is supplemented by the discipline of momentary, conscious recognition of His presence and headship in all the affairs which come and go throughout the day. We become thus more and more sensitive to His gentle pressure upon our hearts that prompts us here, checks us there, as to conduct, as to what we say in our conversation, as to where we go, as to what we buy, as to where we are seen, as to whom we turn to give help, as to which beggar is worthy, as to when to answer and when to keep silent, as to what recreations are wholesome, as to whether to leave the TV on this station or turn to another — and when to turn it off! — as to when to go with an apology for a misspoken word or an act that hurt another.

This is the essence of spiritual-mindedness. There is no end to the room for development here in ever increasing sensitiveness to the Spirit's pressure as a momentary guide through every day. It helps me to think of His guidance as a pressure rather than a voice in my soul. Indeed, it is necessary to recognize that the guidance of the Spirit is meant to assist us primarily with moral judgments. It is not concerned with the prudential thing to do but with the *right* thing to do. It is not concerned with giving us, for their own sake, infallible answers about how to make money in business, or whether it will rain tomorrow, or whether the stock market will go up or down, or the like. It is not a species of necromancy or palm-reading by which our curiosity may be satisfied about things which we need not know, or we may be spared the labor of using our reason and judgment in their sanctified form. But it is given to show us the moral aspect of all such.   The Spirit is interested in helping a man to conduct his business on strictly Christian lines, whether or not that means financial success.   Financial success concerns the Spirit only indirectly as it bears on the businessman's moral standing in the will of God.   This fact gives us our clue as to how to learn the voice of the Spirit.

It is precisely in the matter of "crossing the line," which was treated in the last chapter, that guidance begins. People want spectacular guidance — to avoid taking the train that is going to be wrecked or to choose the right occupation or companion — but they forget that these extraordinary experiences come to those who have built well the foundation of sensitiveness to the Spirit's pressure in the soul in small matters.   The increase of sensitiveness to the voice of the Spirit is in direct proportion to the implicitness of obedience moment by moment.

No man can tell another when he is becoming a glutton, but the Holy Spirit will.   No man can tell another when his sensitiveness is becoming self-centered to the point of enmity against God, but the Holy Spirit always does.   One may be confused in his own thinking as to when religious zeal becomes envy, when the encouraging words of others are being accepted by an inordinate love of praise, when righteous anger gives way to an ugly temper, but into that confusion will come, if we listen, the "still small voice," that gentle pressure of the Spirit in tones of conviction: "This is the way, walk ye in it."   To know when we are exercising leadership for the thrill of power, or when the enjoyment of the presence of one of the opposite sex is becoming a thing of danger or disloyalty, or when the admiration of beauty has shifted to the lustful look — all this is possible only by the guidance of the Spirit.   Our Christian experience will be barren and merely historic unless it is made a living thing through the guidance of the Holy Spirit.   "As many as are led by the Spirit of God, they are the children of God."

A homely illustration may make this whole matter clearer.

As a boy my besetting sin was talking too much. Speech is a gift from God. What would preachers do without it? Yet how easily it gets out of hand — even in sermons! My social life was pretty largely confined to a group of church young people, and our socials were full of fun. I seemed able to talk non-stop in these socials and somehow people would laugh. Still I was trying to be an earnest Christian and this incessant frivolousness began to bother me. It was not that there was anything inherently wrong in what was said; no one was being run down, there were no dirty or even off-color stories, nor were there falsehoods. But the very lightness and silliness of so much that was said sent me home with an awful sense of emptiness. Night after night I came home and prayed about it. Then the next party resulted in the same thing.

At last I became desperate and decided one night to take the bull by the horns. I went early that evening and took a seat back in a corner where I would be able to sit it out in silence. The party gathered and the chatter began. Then someone asked where Cattell was. Somebody else spotted him in a corner. Then the crowd ran over and wanted to know what was the matter — was I ill? Obviously this would not do. This solution was getting too much attention. So I decided to move about a little — just enough to throw off attention and then be quiet. But the move was fatal. A little talk led to more talk, pretty soon I was the life of the party again, and went home with the same empty, aching heart. I cried and prayed over this. Then somehow the Spirit seemed to teach me. He no more wanted to excise fun from a young person's life than He wanted to cut out my tongue. But He did want to control both of them. He seemed to say that if *in the midst of the fun* I would listen, He would speak. And I found it true! I went to the same socials with the same crowd but with a new victory. It was gloriously true that *if I would listen He would speak!* I quickly learned to hear that gentle pressure which seemed to say, "Take care. Let up now. Don't tell that one! Time

to change the subject now." So it would run. Obedience
brought victory and the joy of going to bed and reviewing
an evening in which there had been intense joy but without
loss.

As Sangster said, "*God does guide us.*" And the result is
blessed. If one never had a spectacular experience in his
life, it would be worth everything just to have the kind of
guidance that covers these day-to-day matters. Yet constant obedience in this field brings a growing sensitiveness
to the voice of the Spirit and the larger experiences then become occasionally in order.

The word about guidance in Romans 8 is followed by a
word on the witness of the Spirit. The voice of the Spirit
is the same in both instances. Just as He has a way of making us individually assured of salvation with an inner conviction that leaves no room for doubt, so He speaks in all
His guidance with that same inner voice in conscience,
giving a conviction of certainty. Guidance and conscience
are not the same thing but guidance uses conscience.

There is urgent need of Spirit-guided lives today. One
hesitates to give experiences lest they pose as normative.
But it may be an encouragement to mention one or two to
show how guidance sometimes works out. A new convert
in an Indian village was in deep distress. He had taken
his wife to a Christian gathering for some days and upon
returning found his house looted and the grain supply
nearly gone. It was only a few days until they ate the
last of it. The village was in the midst of a cholera epidemic
so that people were staying indoors and refused to do business. It occurred to the convert that if he just had one
rupee he could get off to the city and get enough grain to
tide them over until the situation was normal again. But
he did not have the rupee. So he and his wife bowed in
their little courtyard for family prayers after the breakfast
of goat's milk, and prayed for one rupee. About the same
time an Indian evangelist was praying for guidance as to
which village he should visit that morning. He rose from

prayer with that inner pressure of the Spirit that he should visit the new convert. Arriving in the village, they talked a while but no word of the need was mentioned. At last the preacher asked the convert if he had any *ghi* for sale. *Ghi* is clarified butter and India's standard shortening. The preachers always like to buy in the villages in the hope of getting things cheaper and purer. The convert answered that he had about a quarter of a rupee's worth. The preacher took it and tied it to his cycle. The conversation went on and nothing was said about paying. When the preacher arose to go, the convert accompanied him to the edge of the village — according to Indian custom. There the preacher asked whether the convert could supply about this amount of *ghi* each week. The goat he had would just make it! So the preacher said he would pay now for four weeks and handed the convert one rupee!

The convert went home, where with his wife he thanked God for answered prayer. And so may we. But I also thank God for a preacher who was sensitive to the leading of the Spirit.

Once I was evangelist for our Young Peoples Conference held on the shores of Lake Erie. One night, after the scheduled service, a spirit of praise came upon the group and one after another began to give words of testimony and thanksgiving. In the course of the praise some girl emphasized deep assurance in her testimony. I felt impressed to start a chorus the author of which had been a remarkable minister in the Friends Church. It had been my honor to follow him in the pastorate where he died. I had seen his widow and two small children through the depression. Then I went to India and had not seen the family for ten years. I understood they had gone East. I hesitated about starting the chorus, for it was old, I had not heard it for a long time, and I did not know whether the young people knew it or not. Three more testimonies passed but the pressure increased. I started the chorus and we sang it twice. During the second time a great strapping young fellow rose, came forward, and gave himself to Christ. I had no idea who he was. Later he testified: "This is the first time I have been happy for two years. I had not thought of my father for a long time until tonight you sang the chorus he wrote. I began to wonder what he would think if he knew the way I had been living." It broke him, and he found Christ. How easy it would have been to have brushed aside that gentle pressure to sing, especially since singing is naturally rather hard for me. But how thankful I have been for obedience at that point.

5

Praying in the Spirit

"The Spirit . . . helpeth our infirmities" (Rom. 8:26). Anyone who can talk or think lightly of his infirmities and feel no compunction about them has scarcely started on the road to holiness. Now what do we mean by "infirmities"? Let it be clear that we do not mean breakdowns, disobediences, and defeats, for they are sin. Infirmity is evident when we are doing our best. When we are active in the most spiritual exercises, just at that point we are conscious of the greatest weakness. "We have this treasure in earthen vessels." The Apostle, after giving the assurance of help from the Spirit, goes on to give an illustration, showing that our greatest weakness is often apparent in the realm of our most spiritual effort, that is, prayer. Not when the flesh is pulling us, but when we are doing the most spiritual thing one can think of, we are most infirm. "For we know not what we should pray for as we ought."

For many the difficulty is simply that they do not pray. "Ye have not, because ye ask not" (James 4:2). I am amazed at how many Christians — even preachers and missionaries — do not have a satisfactory prayer life. Of course, there is a sense in which we are never satisfied with our prayer life. But in another very real sense there can be a satisfactory prayer life. It comes simply from *doing* it. "Prayer," someone has said, "is the thing we talk so much

about and do so little of." I have to confess with shame
how long it was before I experienced any satisfaction in the
matter. I had always prayed and much had come of it,
but there was too much irregularity and too many times of
being deeply convicted of failure. For instance, I found
myself often with a committee, sitting in judgment upon an
erring brother, when I had seen him sagging for many
months before the break came. Yet I had not prayed for
him. This became intensely convicting for me. I can now
humbly testify to what a difference there is, when dealing
with one who has failed of the grace of God, to be able to
say, "Brother, these past two years you have been daily in
my prayers." This gives one spiritual authority which no
appointment to any office can possibly give.

For years I let certain misconceptions rob me of the best
in prayer. The first such misconception was the idea that
I ought not to make prayer a routine, that it should be free
and spiritual and, therefore, I should pray when I felt burdened. The second grew out of reading books where illustrations were given from famous men of prayer who prayed
three, five or eight hours a day. I assumed that if I ever
got to be what I ought to be, I would pray eight hours a day.
Once I set out to put in eight hours. It was the deadest
thing I ever did, just trying to put in time. Needless to say,
I did not stick it out. The third misconception was the
practical expedient of saying to myself that I knew prayer
ought to come first but how could I pray with the pressure
of this cluttered desk on my mind — I would just clear the
desk quickly, and then be able to pray unhurriedly. Needless to say, that never happened.

At long last the answer came. I learned that prayer has
to be a discipline before it can be a joy. There may be a
few people for whom prayer is a sheer delight and the chief
one of life. But for ninety-nine per cent of us this will not
be true. If we merely pray when we feel like it, our prayers
will be very spasmodic. *Prayer has to be a discipline.* There
must be regularity of time and perhaps of place in order

merely to guarantee that we get at it and get it done. Fortunately, this leads to better things as the discipline gives way to joy. Much of the joy grows out of the results. Regular, definite prayer gets regular, definite answers, and these in turn encourage to more prayer.

As to the time element, I found that successful prayer cannot be measured by the clock — it must rather be measured in terms of *unhurriedness*. That is to say, we must have a daily spot where we have a sense of release from every other care — that there is nothing else to do but to speak and to listen to God. So many of our prayers consist of hugely comprehensive sentences lumped together. How often one hears the prayer, "Lord, bless all the missionaries." That way of praying is not characteristic of praying in the unhurried quiet time, where one can allow himself to be led out into detailed petitions. And one needs time sufficient to be able to stop and listen to God. When we are in a hurry we tend to do all the talking. This is an impertinence. Some are afraid to stop saying something before God for fear of wandering thoughts. But where is there a better place to do our serious thinking than in the presence of God?

"We know not what to pray for as we ought." This serious infirmity can only be corrected by taking enough time before God to let the Spirit teach us. A missionary friend of mine told me that he had used a prayer list until it became as mechanical as a rosary. It is not a discrediting of the obvious value of a prayer list to insist that in our unhurried quiet time we must get to the place where we transcend all mechanics and where on any given day the Spirit may lift something out of the list or inject something not yet written, with a gentle pressure which brings that item into the center of focus, making it the burden of the day, sometimes along with, and sometimes to the exclusion of, the other items on the list.

It is here that we can best begin our day's work. There is no rule which will fit everyone, but for most of us this

unhurriedness can only be had at the cost of the discipline
of early rising. Not only do we thus begin our day's work
by getting help from God in planning the day, but we begin
our day with the most serious part of our work.

It is here that we wrestle with our problems most effectively. We hold them before God, seeking how to petition
about them and seeking for the divine answer. It is part
of the discipline of faith to keep holding them before God
day after day, not forgetting or growing careless even though
there seems no answer vouchsafed at all. Often this continues to the day when we have to have an answer. But
how preciously faithful is the Holy Spirit. Again and again
as one waits before God that day, the answer comes, sometimes as a deep conviction of rightness attaching to a solution which had been vaguely suggesting itself through the
days, and sometimes as a brand new idea like a bolt from
the blue.

It is in the quiet, too, that we intercede for others — our
family, our friends, the people of God, those with whom we
labor, our neighbors everywhere. For most of us this list
is so long as to have to be spread over the week. Our list
may include those who are under temptation or are failing,
but it should also include those who are not. From the
Apostle Paul I have learned that we must pray for the best
people in the church as well as the failures. All need the
undergirding of our prayers to guard them from the attacks
of the enemy and to sustain them in Christian living. Too
often we pray for an erring one until the prayer is answered.
Then we breathe a sigh of relief and mark that one off the
list.

Probably the deepest lesson about prayer came to me from
Dr. O. Hallesby's book entitled *Prayer.* He defined prayer
as simply confessing our helplessness to God. As long as we
can still suggest to God ways and means by which He might
answer our petitions we may be communing with God but
not really praying. But when we get to the extremity of not
being able even to imagine how God might do it, then we

are ready to pray. Dr. Hallesby illustrates his point with the case of praying for the salvation of three men. One is a pretty good sort of fellow, a second is worse, and the third is so sinful as to seem hopeless. We pray for them all. We can see rather easily how God could save the first. So we pray, as we think, with much assurance for his salvation. For the second, we pray, but faith is more difficult. The third seems doubtful. It is hard to keep praying for him, for we just cannot see how God could possibly reach him. Dr. Hallesby insists that we are really in a position to pray only for the latter. For prayer is prayer only when we are confessing our helplessness. This truth revolutionized my prayer life.

We do not know what to pray for. James suggests, as a second reason for unanswered prayer, the fact that we "ask amiss, that ye may consume it upon your lusts" (James 4:3). It is amazing how many of our petitions are selfish. What a task it is to get the mind of the Lord and pray actually according to the will of the Father. The classic illustration of this is that of Monica's praying for her son Augustine that he might be prevented from going from Carthage to Rome where she feared he would become yet more profligate and heretical. God answered the prayer, not by keeping Augustine from Rome but by sending him on to Milan. There He brought about his conversion.[1] Monica wanted her boy saved. This the Lord did, but He did not do it by the means which she suggested. What a great quantity of our praying is concerned with suggesting to God ways and means for doing His work! We ought, on the contrary, to be confessing our helplessness.

The writer to the Hebrews urges that another condition for prayer is faith — a believing not only that God is, but that "he is a rewarder of them that diligently seek him" (Heb. 11:6). One day I stopped on my way home from the university to make a pastoral call in a home where there was sickness. The house was a mere shack, out of square and

1. *The Confessions of St. Augustine*, Book V.

leaning so that it had to be braced with a pole. The ne'er-do-well father was in the sawdust business. He always talked to me about the great future there was in sawdust. Meanwhile the family was in poverty. The mother was a saint. I have rarely seen anyone else come through such a continual barrage of trouble with such a constantly sweet spirit. Most of her children had gone bad; some were in institutions. Her only comfort in life was an eight-year-old boy who came to church with her. Now he was sick — measles, pneumonia, and brain fever. If he got well, the doctor said he would doubtless be mentally impaired.

When I entered the room the mother was kneeling by the bedside with her hand on the boy's forehead. Two women from the church sat silently in the room. The mother's face was an agony to see. Too moved to weep, too hurt to speak, her prayer was just a groan. I looked at the boy. His drawn face had the marks of death. I lingered in the home a long while thinking the end might come while I was there. Then I thought: "Now, just what have I to give this mother?" I thought of the three classes at the university I had attended that day. Was there anything from them that would help? In Philosophy of Religion we had tried to decide whether there was a God or not. Should I raise that question with this mother? In Contemporary Philosophy we had talked about Nietzsche's conception of God. Could that help this mother? In Educational Philosophy we had tried to decide whether there were any fixed standards in the world. Could I anchor this mother to a world of complete relativism? What should I do? What would you do? There was only one thing left to do. I knelt and prayed.

To make a long story short, that boy today is in his right mind, well and strong, and the last I knew he was preaching the Gospel. What is the explanation? I think I know all the naturalistic answers that are supposed to be given. The university saw to that! But just the same there burns down in my soul a conviction that God answers prayer. "Men hold opinions, but convictions hold men."

I must not leave the impression, however, that the validity of praying depends upon striking or phenomenal results. This is decidedly not true. But specific praying in matters large and small gets specific answers. And when we experience this, we experience the glow of reality of holy living.

William Penn said of George Fox: "But above all he excelled in prayer. The most awful, living, reverent frame I ever felt or beheld, I must say, was his in prayer. And truly it was a testimony he knew, and lived nearer to the Lord than other men; for they that know him most will see most reason to approach him with reverence and fear."[2]

O God: Grant me a little of that!

2. William Penn: *Preface* to George Fox's *Journal*.

6

The Unity of the Spirit

No man liveth unto himself, but sin is the attempt to do it. When we are born again it is not into an orphanage but into a family. We are given cleansing on the specific condition that we walk in the light and have fellowship one with another. Of the two Greek words commonly used in the New Testament for the church, it is strange that in common practice *ecclesia* should have taken the ascendancy and *koinonia* should have faded. It may be because *ecclesia* could be identified with organization and organization gets the help of the world. But fellowship is a different matter: this sinful world is against that. To build the church as a *koinonia* or fellowship is far more costly. But have we really a right to call anything a church that is not a fellowship? Certainly not with New Testament justification, for to conceive of the church in terms of the body and the bride of Christ is to use figures which are implicit with the idea of fellowship. Fellowship is of the very spirit or character of the Body of Christ. One of the most serious criticisms made against the "holiness sects" is their predisposition to strife and division. For holiness the message of I Corinthians 13 is one of the fundamentals.

The Ecumenical movement appears, superficially, to be headed in the direction of unity. Yet one wonders whether we have not put the cart before the horse. The place to begin is in the local congregation. How can worldwide church unity be achieved if in thousands of local congregations the solidarity of Christian fellowship has given way to the atomizing influence of dissension, pride, jealousy, and division? You can build a bridge on a foundation of solid stone, but not on one of incohesive sand. The enemy knows this and directs his major attacks against the fellowship of believers. Let us look at four case studies in the early church in which the fellowship was threatened and see what was done about it.

Case Number One. This was a matter of *administrative inefficiency* (Acts 6:1-8). It grew out of the alleged neglect of certain widows in the daily bread-line. The solution of a problem in administration is really not very difficult and so the enemy almost never lets the problem remain simple and uncomplicated. Typically, in this instance, the administrative problem was thrown into a different emotional gear by involving it with race prejudice. To get up much enthusiasm for a quarrel over the breakdown of the system of distribution would be difficult. It would be too easy to see what should be done and simply do it. But the minute you mention Jews and Greeks — put in a dash of race or color or theology — you can count on partisanship at once and the imputing of sinister motives. That makes a *good* quarrel! How often differences over administrative procedure are cast in the shadow of doctrinal unsoundness or moral aspersion. It is quite certain that had the Apostles been slow to find the solution to their administrative problem, after a very short time the "widow issue" would have been overshadowed by an acute racial dispute, with the slinging of labels, discrimination, side-taking, and selfishness.

Happily the Apostles had the spiritual insight to keep the issue unclouded by secondary factors. Along with this a true humility led them to divide responsibility and surrender temporal power. The refusal to do these two things has wrecked fellowship in many a subsequent case. Suppose the Apostles had suggested one to another that certain elements in the church were trying to get both power and money in their control, and that instead of all Apostles preaching, certain ones henceforth should be set free for office work, to give more time to supervision and eliminate abuses and keep the ambitious people in their places?

Have we the vision of these men who renounced these natural and carnal impulses, who shared responsibility, who released to other trustworthy hands the administration, but insisted that a growing church needed above all else a larger body of spiritual leaders free to give themselves to prayer and the Word? Some will protest their willingness to share responsibility provided they can find men who are really trustworthy. This is a point well taken. Sharing responsibility with carnal and untrustworthy men may indeed be disastrous. But if men of proper spiritual qualifications are not at hand we will do well to ask ourselves why. Perhaps the reason is that we have for so long failed to give spiritual leadership, having been so fully occupied with serving tables, that now, looking about us, we cannot find "seven men of honest report, full of the Holy Ghost and wisdom, whom we may appoint over this business."

One cannot emphasize too much the necessity of doing spiritual work in spiritual ways and with spiritual tools. For instance, we say that we believe in prayer. We say that prayer is more important than anything else. But how many of us actually put it first in our programs?

It was my privilege for twenty years to belong to a fellowship in a mission in India that literally tried to put prayer first. We met for as many days as a situation required, often for three or four days. We gave ourselves to the Word and to prayer — and prayed as long as we were burdened to do so. No one worried whether we had better get on with "business." *Prayer* was our business.

Prayer is our first business. The Apostolic pattern of spiritual leaders giving themselves "to prayer and to the ministry of the word" is an absolute necessity for spiritual growth in the church. We pray for pastors and "deacons" to be raised up to help us. School training is not enough for these. They must be "of honest report, full of the Holy Ghost and wisdom." And for getting such workers, praying is better than advertising.

It is amazing how quickly the so-called "business" gets done if it has been saturated with prayer. Furthermore, we do not settle major problems by majority vote. Quakers state their principle thus: Where Friends cannot go together, we will not go at all. Disagreement does not call for a struggle — it calls for more prayer. The unity of the Spirit maintained among us in this prayer fellowship is absolutely priceless.

Case Number Two. This case issued in the Jerusalem Council (Acts 15:1-35). The question at issue concerned not administrative procedure but rather the Gospel: is the Gospel for Gentiles or only for Jews; and if it be for Gentiles, must they conform to Jewish rites and customs?

The first significant fact revealed in the solution to this threatened rupture in the church is that a group representative of the whole church settled the matter. How fortunate that Antioch did not start off on a line of its own, irrespective of the feelings of Jerusalem! How fortunate that it had not yet occurred to Paul and Barnabas that they could start the Pauline church at Antioch on lines of freedom for Gentiles while the Petrine church at Jerusalem was abandoned to Judaizing tendencies — a course of action usually covered with the platitude that different temperaments call for different types of churches.

The second significant fact in the solution is that all parties recognized the sovereignty of the Holy Spirit. The tests made were somewhat pragmatic. The question was: In what way is the Holy Spirit actually at work today in the world? Paul and Barnabas brought in field evidence. It thus became obvious that the Holy Spirit was actually at work among Gentiles, conferring upon them the same spiritual blessings without Jewish rites as had been received by Jewish Christians. Hence, the decision said in substance: It is our task to co-operate with the Holy Spirit *where*, and *as*, He is at work.

The third significant fact is that the Council listened to the Scriptures. In summing up the case, James quoted Scripture, showing that work among Gentiles was to be expected. The same Holy Spirit who wrote the Book is the One who may be observed working in any given field. He never contradicts Himself. If a true work of the Spirit is going on in any given place it will be amply corroborated by the Scriptures. The Scriptures are thus our rule of faith because they reveal the mind of the Spirit.

A fourth significant fact revealed in this case is that, having once settled upon the main issue as being determined by the Holy Spirit through His Word and His obvious work, all were willing to be generous to the feelings and even to the prejudices of others in less important secondary matters. The four restrictions passed on to the Gentile churches by James' decision were definitely concessions to Jewish feeling. Two of the items were important — idolatry and fornication — and Paul was satisfied that these would be cared for even in Christian teaching without the aid of Jewish influence. But the matters of certain meats, blood, and strangulation, Paul likewise felt sure, would fade out by their own inherent unimportance if left unopposed. In Galatians he does not mention them at all in his review of this case; he speaks rather of having been urged to take collections from the Gentiles for the poor, which he was careful to do. We, too, must learn the graciousness of allowing liberty to others in non-essentials, being assured that if we co-operate with the Holy Spirit these non-essentials will fall off like so many dead leaves in due time.

Suppose, however, that the leaders at Jerusalem had failed to come to the decision which they did, and had gone along with the Judaizers. What then should Paul and Barnabas have done? Should they have gone along with a position which violated their conscience in order to preserve unity or should they have separated? This is an important question in our day when separation has become almost a fetish with some fundamentalists. If the denomination to which one belongs has admitted into its leadership men who have departed from the evangelical faith, are true members obliged to leave?

In the first place, let it be clear that the answer must be scriptural. It must not be born either of expediency or compromise. We must see the Scriptures whole and interpret them with a sound exegesis. Precisely because of this love of the Scriptures one cannot accept a simple emphasis on "separation" based on a text like II Corinthians 6:17, "Wherefore come out from among them and be ye separate, saith the Lord," as applying to this problem. Such an application is bad exegesis, and it fails to take the Scriptures whole. It is bad exegesis because the text, taken in context, refers to separation from the heathen; to apply the text to contemporary denominations involves one in judging that these churches are pagan, which is quite wrong. If a denomination officially changes its creed to a unitarian or anti-Christian one, then the case is clear. Official creeds, however, are rarely changed. Rather, leaders change, or views of leaders change. And when such leaders are not disciplined, the church represents a mixture of views. The situation is further complicated when some of the leaders do not believe that they have rejected Christ. They are sincere — however mistaken — in their belief that their new knowledge is what a Christian ought to hold. In this situation it is beyond our power to judge which men are non-Christian, or heathen. Therefore, no simple application of this text is possible.

Beyond this is the matter of the total teaching of Scripture on this point. Frank Colquhoun has done us a great service in gathering together the range of Scripture teaching on this subject in his book entitled *The Fellowship of the Spirit*.

From such a study it is clear that the New Testament has two complementary messages. There is a clear-cut word on separation from sin, evil, and unbelief. At the same time there is an immense amount of Scripture devoted to the necessity of keeping the unity of the Spirit among believers. We tend to champion the one truth to the exclusion of the other, instead of holding them together in the living tension which God intended. Our practical problem is increased by the difficulty of telling for certain who is a Christian and who is not. Undoubtedly there are times when separation is called for and becomes a virtue. But there are also times when to suffer through a bad situation is redemptive.

Here is another instance where we are shut up to the guidance of the Holy Spirit to make application of a general truth (held in a tension between two poles) to any given particular case. And we must allow freedom to individuals to get that guidance for themselves. Wholesale condemnation of those who do not feel led to leave their particular denomination, even though some of its leaders have in some cases become apostate, is a judgment which we are not at liberty to make. Likewise, the plea that the teaching of Scripture on unity makes it wrong for anyone ever to separate from a bad situation is false. But since so much of Scripture deals with the need of fellowship being maintained even at great cost, let us separate, when we must, without gloating, rejoicing or hilarity — but with tears. It is never God's best — no matter who is to blame. And let the doors for reunion always be kept open. On the other hand, since the Scriptures enjoin hatred for evil, let those who remain in unsatisfactory situations, in order to try to redeem them, never be overcome by evil or made to grow insensitive to it; let them maintain a good testimony to the end.

A further aid in difficult situations is to recognize that fellowship has different levels, two principal ones being the *consultative* and the *active*. Failure to recognize these has led to vast quantities of needless suffering. The usual emphasis upon unity is that it must be *total* — especially in these days of ecumenicity. This requires that both consultation and action be united. But widely differing theological views often call for programs of action which not only differ but sometimes counteract each other. To force these programs to operate at the same place and time merely means that each cancels the other out. This is not of the essence of love or of unity. It is possible that a kind of separation may be more Christian and more loving and a better expression of unity than forced proximity. Separating into two different areas, for the working out of divergent programs, with unity maintained at a consultative level, often provides the fullest scope to each for its expression. This course provides for mutual respect, which is of the essence of unity.

Case Number Three. This case is much more difficult but at the same time of great importance to us, for it concerns the type of difference which is most common among us and spoils fellowship more frequently than any other. It is a clear-cut case of *personality clash* (Acts 15:36-41).

There is a sense in which Paul and Barnabas won the day at Jerusalem, and they would be less than human if they did not return to Antioch with a deep sense of gratitude to God for victory. And Satan would be less than what he is if he did not try to twist this sense of gratitude into a sense of personal triumph. It is a very dangerous thing to be on the winning side of a contention, even when one is right. It does something inside of one which must be kept under control if one would escape disaster. For there is something terribly infectious about differences and broken fellowship. It may be that Paul and Barnabas both came away with a sense of triumph, quite legitimate in the beginning, which Satan twisted until, when he precipitated (as he usually does) a fresh situation in which difference was threatened between the two partners in victory, the very gratitude for victory became a sense of personal triumph which made it difficult for either to become a yielder, and both were caught in a position where they felt obliged to get the victory again. Perhaps this is a false judgment of their case, but it certainly is true of a multitude of clashes in our day, where one victory calls for another at almost any cost. The devil springs this trap with frightful regularity.

Now look at the personalities involved. They were direct opposites. Paul was intense and rigid, whereas Barnabas was calm and generous. Barnabas, whose real name was Joses, was called Barnabas by the disciples in order to describe his character as a "son of consolation." Paul's treatment of John Mark was much more consistent with his temperament than with his memory, for had he remembered, he would have realized that when he was a young Christian it was Barnabas who stood up for him and got him admitted to the Jerusalem fellowship, when the other Christians were so afraid of Paul as to have nothing to do with him. It was Barnabas who realized the possibilities in this young convert and brought him from Tarsus to Antioch to start him in Christian service. It was Barnabas also who commenced as the leader of a mission consisting of "Barnabas and Paul," and who later developed his young friend until he gracefully reversed the order and made Paul the leader in so inconspicuous a way as to leave no more trace of the transition than the mere switching of the phrase to "Paul and Barnabas." God give us more Barnabases along with our Pauls!

Paul was a giant character. He was capable of a terrific self-discipline. Often this made him seem severe in his dealings with others. He was God's man for the hour because the church was at a point of development which called for a severe discipline. There is something towering, something magnificent, something colossal, about Paul. Aside from the Lord Jesus Christ, he, judged by his effect upon history, is easily the world's greatest man. Christian leaders have found his life a never-ending source of inspiration and encouragement. But it does not necessarily follow that he would have been easy to live with. There are a good many great missionaries today with whom I would just as leave not have to live! My guess is that it would have been a good deal more comfortable to be stationed with Barnabas than with Paul.

Who was right and who was wrong in this affair about

John Mark? I am sure that only God really knows. Attempts are often made to show that good really came out of this, perhaps more good than if they had remained united. It is possible that God overruled this for good and certainly some good did come out of it. But to say that more good came from separation than from unity is pure conjecture and I find it less convincing the longer I study this incident. I have a growing suspicion that this case must be faced as a minor tragedy. The whole experience clashes with Paul's deeper insights. Whoever was right or wrong, it remains true that the word translated "sharp contention" is the Greek word from which by transliteration comes our English word "paroxysm," and Paul says in I Corinthians 13:5 that love does not have paroxysms ("love is not provoked"). One of these men may have been right, but neither can lay much claim to love at that moment. Even mild people like Barnabas can be most stubborn and unyielding on occasion. Furthermore, it is hard to reconcile this incident with the teaching of Paul, elaborated in so many epistles: "Submitting yourselves one to another in the fear of God." I believe they both were wrong.

Suppose that Paul had said, "Well, brother Barnabas, I am convinced that taking this boy with us will only lead to disaster again. I have no confidence in him. But I admit that you have made something out of very unlikely material before and possibly you are right about John. It seems mere weakness and foolishness to me, but if you insist I am surely willing and we'll do the best we can for him. So let him come along."

And suppose Barnabas had answered, "Now, brother Paul, I really do feel there is a future for this boy. He is weak, but I believe he has learned a lesson. I feel strongly that he ought to have another chance and that we can afford to take some risks in giving it. But on the other hand, I quite realize your point that our work is most difficult and beset with awful attacks from the enemy and we must be a party of perfect unity and courage in the Holy Ghost. So I won't insist on John going with us this time. If you don't share my conviction, then let us drop the matter, for we cannot afford to have anything come between us. Perhaps we can send John Mark on some other errand where he can prove himself again."

Suppose it had been thus. Would there have been any need for a paroxysm? And could not love and mutual submission have triumphed? And could Paul and Barnabas not then have entered into a prayer fellowship in which the Spirit would have shown them clearly what to do with John Mark, bringing them to unity in the matter, just as He guided them through so many other difficult situations? Could two men who had such marvelous experiences of divine guidance in other matters, and who failed to get it when their personalities clashed, not get it here also if their mutual submission became as deep as their united surrender to God had been on other occasions where guidance was forthcoming?

Indeed, it would seem that this tragedy was used of the Spirit to mark a turning point in the life of Paul. It is curious that in the Book of Acts there is no mention of the Spirit's guidance in the first missionary journey, nor up until this incident. But from here on one runs into such expressions as: "forbidden of the Holy Ghost to preach the Word in Asia" (16:6), "assayed to go into Bithynia but the Spirit suffered them not" (16:7), "Paul purposed in the Spirit . . . to go to Jerusalem" (19:21), "bound in the Spirit to Jerusalem" (20:23), beside numerous references to guidance in a vision in the night (16:10, 18:9, 23:11, 27:22-26). It seems that Paul grasped a new way of handling personality clashes, for in addition to the guidance recorded above he also came to emphasize again and again his doctrine of mutual submission, crowning it with his Hymn to Love (I Cor. 13). Our mistakes also can be made a blessing to us if we learn the Lord's lessons from them.

Our churches need a great revival of preaching this doctrine of mutual submission. What a difference would be found in relations between Christian workers if this doctrine were practiced.

Another relationship where personality clashes are most common and the doctrine of mutual submission specially needed is marriage. The Christian view of marriage as a fellowship is no new thing. "And the Lord God said, It is not good that man should be alone; I will make him an helpmeet for him" (Gen. 2:18). To find this written at a time when womanhood was degraded and regarded as a chattel, polygamy accepted, and biological necessity was the supreme motivation for marriage, gives it the ring of the genuine revealed Word of God. The New Testament delineations of this relationship make it a fellowship based on mutual submission defined in terms of obedience and love. The wife's obedience is safe because of the husband's love. His love is not taken advantage of because of the wife's obedience. This is the ideal. Neither of these is to be identified with infatuation or natural attraction. Both obedience and love as set forth by the Apostles are voluntary choices — choices which must be kept in operation by continuously willing them.

The beautiful fellowship which obtains in ideal marriage would under ideal circumstances come about through natural compatibility. That means that temperamentally, spiritually, sexually, and mentally the couple would find themselves in complete harmony, complementing without antagonizing, coordinating without friction. But in real life this rarely occurs. The achievement of this necessary fellowship therefore becomes a matter not of natural attraction nor of natural compatibility but of redemptive love. In all redemption, love is a volition and the instrument is a cross. And in redemption there is less interest in those couples who "were made for each other" than in those who by a cross have made their fellowship across the chasms of natural incompatibility.

Some incompatibilities are natural and some are voluntary. Unfaithfulness, nagging, tyranny, self-indulgence and the like must be catalogued as of the voluntary type. Voluntary pursuit of friction-making or fellowship-breaking characteristics is a matter of guilt and can only be righted with repentance and restitution. Involuntary or natural incompatibilities are often to be forgiven because they are unrecognized, and they are therefore to be bridged with a voluntary cross by the other partner. But when one is informed about his involuntary faults and he fails to make a consistent effort to correct them, he becomes guilty of breaking fellowship. The one possessing the offensive trait must earnestly and consistently try to correct or eradicate it. It may have the tenacity of longtime habit. The more deeply intrenched it has become the greater the cross. And for the other partner there is a cross in the bearing of this antagonism.

Much of modern thought refers all marital difficulties to poor sexual adjustment. I should not want to minimize the importance of sexual adjustment, and I am aware that in the majority of cases where there is marital unhappiness there is also a bad sexual adjustment. But bad sexual adjustment is not so much cause as it is symptom. The root of the difficulty is ultimately selfishness — a spiritual matter calling for spiritual treatment. This spiritual disease has a striking way of expressing itself symptomatically in the sex life. Any couple failing to achieve full sex harmony should at once (barring some physical disability) recognize that this is a sure symptom of a basic selfishness which will increasingly declare itself in a constantly enlarging group of incompatibilities. Whether these incompatibilities take the form of prudery, self-indulgence, notionate modesty, prejudice, or bestiality, the common denominator is selfishness. Of course, ignorance may be a factor, but that is scarcely excusable in this day of excellently and frankly written books on sex in marriage.

When we recognize that the root difficulty in marriage is spiritual rather than physical our vision as to the cure is clarified. Where selfishness is the root, the Cross is the cure.

And when that cure is operative there will be sexual adjustment, and far more. Where selfishness is crucified all marital frictions should give way to adjustment. There are no impossibilities for the Cross.

Too many young people think of marriage as a matter of getting rather than giving. Courtship has been a happy and flattering experience of getting attention and what not — even flowers and candy. But marriage as a getting is doomed to failure. Only marriage as a giving succeeds. Marriage is a stewardship. When either party indulges in a feeling of possessiveness toward the other he is forgetting that both belong primarily to God.

From the wife is demanded an obedience as thoroughgoing as that which the true Church gives to Christ. From the husband is demanded love that is self-giving, even as Christ gave Himself for the Church. The Christian way is not merely to avoid divorce, or to act as though marriage were some kind of endurance contest. Rather, the Christian way is to practice the *will to love*, even to a cross which triumphs in resurrection power and newness of life.

An objection to the New Testament conception of marriage is that it is highly idealistic, and suitable only where both parties fully measure up to the standard. That is to say, where, and only where, a husband loves and gives himself for his wife as Jesus gave Himself for the Church is it safe for a wife to give implicit obedience, and conversely, only where a wife gives such obedience is it safe for a man to lay himself out in selfless humility, treating her with honor and love and without a trace of bitterness, risking his standing and right as head of the home. But here is exactly the virtue of the Christian program. The Kingdom does not wait for a perfect world for initiation. It is within you. Nor did God wait for perfectly obedient men before He instituted redemption. He laid Himself out in a prodigality of love that wins. He took the chance of its being spurned. That is the Cross. And Christian marriage must have its cross. It cannot wait for, nor be limited to, perfectly adjusted couples. It is a way of redemption. And the disillusionment and conflict and unhappiness in such a large percentage of homes today is just such a field as that in which God delights to make His redemption valid.

But what about the cruel husband — perhaps the drunken husband — who squanders his money, endangers the security of the home, perhaps loses property and beats his wife? Shall she obey him? This is difficult. One sympathizes wholeheartedly with the wife — that is, if it was not her nagging, or easy spending, or frigidity, or hypocrisy, or unfaithfulness which drove him to drink. But granted that the case is clearly one of an innocent and faithful wife victimized by a cruel and self-indulgent husband, it is not easy to ask her to submit. Modern ideas about divorce make fairly easy the ways out. But the cross is not easy. We shall have to make up our minds as to what we are looking for: an easy escape or a victorious and redemptive love. Love is not a mere sentiment. It is strong as steel. I have seen it step in with winning tenderness but with iron firmness in a financial situation where mortgages were about to be foreclosed because of a husband's drunken waste. I doubt whether any man can tell a woman how to do this but I have often seen it accomplished by sheer divine grace. I have stood alongside many a woman who was treading this way of a cross when I could do no more for her than to lend her the moral support she needed to be strong where strength was called for and to give encouragement where love was tempted to give way to bitterness. There seems to be something innate in the constitution of women who are fully surrendered, to which God's Spirit is able to give guidance for carrying difficult crosses, holding firmness in a chalice of humility, exercising obedience and also leadership. Perhaps this is why God created woman a sort of paradox.

What does it mean for a husband to give himself, as Christ gave Himself for the Church, to a nagging wife? This problem of nagging and petty strife is sometimes more pressing than the problem of glaring unfaithfulness because of its proximity. Burning at the stake is no more severe than the Chinese water-dripping form of torture. Great temptations call forth our reserves of energy and attention, but the sins which most easily beset us are those which so continually din our souls as to produce a sort of coma. Thus a man who would loath adultery with all his soul may be guilty of breaking fellowship in his home by merely failing to hold his tongue. It is doubtful whether Christ's victory can be held to be any greater when He prayed for the forgiveness of men who were cruelly pounding nails through His sensitive hands, than when He kept silence before the taunts of the soldiers.

How can one duplicate that marvelous poise which knew when to answer Pilate and when to meet his questions with silence? How easy it would have been for Jesus to have escaped crucifixion by being silent when He was asked whether He was a King and whether He was the Son of God? In His answers one sees more of that transparent character of His. He never sacrificed His essential nature, nor position, nor truthfulness. How marvelously absent in Him was self-seeking and self-vindication. Just so, the Christian husband cannot sacrifice his essential headship of the family. But he will not try to maintain his position by any self-seeking. It may be necessary to rebuke a nagging, selfish spirit, as when Jesus was confronted with Peter's boasts or James and John's desire for eminence or the disciples' loss of faith, but the rebuke must be given with a humility that is willing to wash feet. Jesus never surrendered His Headship of the Divine Family — the Church. "Ye call me Master and well." Yet fellowship replaces subserviency in His subjects. "I have not called you servants, but friends."

Nagging — and this may be done by husband as well as wife — is a difficult problem because of its pettiness. It calls for large doses of silence without sullenness. But no man or woman can live in a perpetual silence, for no home can be a vacuum. And often when one thinks he is giving the "soft answer that turneth away wrath," it starts a fresh hail.

Then he is apt to wish he had been silent, and he becomes confused as to when to be silent and when to speak. Here again is need for that experience, real to Jesus, of the momentary guidance of the Spirit of God. There is a still small voice, a quiet, tender pressure which the Spirit exerts upon our souls, if we are sensitive to it, which reveals the way to take in just such practical moments as this. Blessed is the man or woman who is so sensitive and has learned to hear that voice during a torrent of abuse. The ideal, of course, is for the offending party to be converted and cleansed of this nagging spirit, for a nagging spirit is not to be found in a Spirit-filled heart. But we are now considering the way of the Cross in non-ideal circumstances. Suppose the wife will not submit to God for this cleansing. How then will love go into action? The Spirit is prepared to chart the course of silence and kindly speech.

Love wins in the long run, but there is a price to pay. Otherwise it would not be a cross. Jesus' soft answers did not stop Pilate from making his choice nor keep the spikes from being driven. So in a home, the most completely Spirit-guided and Spirit-filled life may not win through to ideal harmony. But such a life will maintain the witness not only of a clear conscience but of a soul kept free from bitterness. For the one so led, and so keeping silence, and so answering, will find that where those answers proceed from love rather than from self they leave no residue of bitterness in the heart. Paul must have had this nagging situation in mind when he gave the injunction, "Husbands, love your wives, and be not bitter against them" (Col. 3:19). This is the practical application of the more general word, "Love suffereth long and is kind" (I Cor. 13:4).

Case Number Four. This concerns failure and rebuke (Gal. 2:11-16). Peter had failed to be true to his vision, and Paul administers rebuke. Failure to rebuke wrong or to rebuke in love with a view to restoration rather than condemnation is, I think, a general weakness in the church. In this case of Peter and Paul, rebuke seems to have been not only faithfully administered but gratefully received. Whether this is to the credit of the loving spirit in which Paul gave it or of the meekness of Peter's spirit in receiving it, one cannot say. That Peter received his reproof in the right spirit may be inferred from Paul's account in Galatians and from a note at the end of Peter's second epistle, where he refers to Paul's epistles "in which are some things hard to be understood." In education and mental caliber the two Apostles stood miles apart, but not in spirit. Peter's loyalty to the brother who talks over his head is clearly evident when he says of these same difficult writings that the "unlearned and unstable wrest [them], as they do also the other Scriptures, unto their own destruction." There is not a trace here of bitterness for a past rebuke. And in the Galatian letter Paul speaks of Peter as having a commission to the Jews equal to that of Paul's to the Gentiles, thus affirming his deep respect for Peter.

Brothers in the faith ought to hold one another up to their best. For this the word of reproof given in love and meekness is necessary. How often after a brother has fallen we say, "Well, I just knew that would come." If so, why did we not give a kindly word of warning? This grace is sadly needed in our time. With it goes the necessity of a deep identification with Christ that will enable us to take a rebuke with patience, meekness, and without bitterness.

But what if the rebuke is unjust or given with censoriousness? First of all, remember that we never have anything to lose by making such a thrust the occasion of deep heart-searching. If it is false we have lost nothing. If there is any truth in it and we mend the matter, we have gained. If we either vocally or in our minds fly instantly to defense and marshall arguments against a rebuke, we lose great benefit. Let the searching take place first. And mark you, let it be a searching of heart for things needing to be made right rather than a searching for bits of goodness with which to offset the rebuke or to prove it unjust, and certainly rather than a searching for evil in the person who administered the rebuke so that we can justify ourselves "tit for tat." Rebuke is the occasion for one of the deepest testings of the reality of our surrender.

An Indian evangelist of note was considerably used of God in our Mission. At a later date he was called to conduct a "jungle camp meeting." Throughout the week, however, it was apparent that something was wrong and the evangelist had no message. On the closing night he was trying to work up a testimony meeting, but it was difficult because there had been little blessing that week. One of our preachers rose to give a testimony, but he was instantly and rudely stopped by the evangelist and forced to sit down. He took his rebuke meekly and without offense. After the meeting the preacher trudged homeward with a heavy heart and greatly tempted. In front of his house around a tree was a mud platform, and there he began to sit down when suddenly in the moonlight he recognized a coiled cobra on that very spot. He looked up in humble thanksgiving to God for deliverance from the snake — and then he recognized its symbolism. He more profoundly thanked God for deliverance from Satan, who was tempting him.

The evangelist, it was soon discovered, had come to us stained with adultery. Of course he had no message. He had also been an open target for the accusations whispered to him by men who were against the preacher who had earlier exposed sin in their lives. It is safe to trust our reputation to God!

Here, then, are some ways in which Satan would break fellowship but in them all there is a way of victory and *victory means maintaining fellowship!*

One of the most beautiful stories in church history has been little publicized. It concerns the little community of Moravians whom Count Zinzendorff gathered on his estate. Before long these earnest Christians fell into terrible dissension. The Count recognized that dissension would be fatal. Accordingly, he called the people together and in discussion and prayer it was settled that, first, they would talk only about the things about which they agreed, and, secondly, that they would give themselves to prayer and to the spread of the Gospel. There was undertaken a round of prayer with at least one person and generally many people in the place of prayer every hour of the twenty-four. This prayer meeting continued unbroken for more than a hundred years, and resulted in the great Moravian missionary enterprise whose zeal and consecration have been without parallel anywhere. Here is the way to fellowship, to unity, and to union.

7

A Definition of Love

John Wesley answered his detractors by saying that his teaching on Christian perfection simply meant "loving God with all our heart, mind, soul, and strength."[1] This is the summary of all we have been saying in this book.

There was an odd bishop who sometimes went about his diocese in disguise to see what his clergy were doing. He came to the back door of a rectory one day, dressed as a tramp, and asked the vicar's wife for a hand-out. She used the opportunity for a little missionary effort and began by asking the poor man how many commandments there were. "Eleven," he replied. "Ten," she corrected. The next morning being Sunday, the bishop appeared at the church and preached. Looking meaningfully into the eyes of the vicar's wife he announced his text: "And a new commandment I give unto you, that ye love one another."

The Rev. Charles Jefferson in a sermon on "The New Commandment" says that he searched over two hundred volumes of sermons and found not one single sermon on this subject. Yet it is the "greatest thing in the world." Church history indicates that there has been a paucity of preaching on this subject. Every preacher ought to read Drummond's great sermon two or three times a year and preach constantly its emphasis.

1. John Wesley, *A Plain Account of Christian Perfection*, p. 62.

The Apostle Paul said: "The fruit of the Spirit is love, joy, peace, longsuffering, gentleness, goodness, faith, meekness and temperance" (Gal. 5:22, 23).

One often hears this text read with the word fruit given in the plural, as though the things listed from love to temperance were so many apples, pears, peaches and bananas growing from the same tree. This is not only incorrect but beclouds a real insight into the deeper meaning of the text. An apple tree may have fruit which varies in size, in color, perfection, etc., but through all runs the same fundamental quality which leads us to call its fruit apples. *The fruit of the Spirit is love.* But love, like other great words, is frequently misunderstood, used in senses which fragment its meaning, and toned down to mere sentimentality. But love is a strong word. There is within it a wealth of meaning, powerful and comprehensive. The Apostle Paul is at pains to have us get its full connotation and so to his statement that the "fruit of the Spirit is love" he adds what is virtually a definition of love. It is as though he said, "The fruit of the Spirit is love, which is. . . ." Then follow eight definitive terms, one fourth of which are terms of feeling and three fourths of which are terms of action. This mathematical ratio is important, especially since there is such a tendency for the term love to degenerate in common usage into mere sentiment. There is a vast difference between love as seen in the infatuation of an adolescent pair, and love as seen in a middle-aged couple one of whom has become a permanent invalid and a constant care to the other. There, love as a sentiment has become love in action.

The six terms used by Paul to define love as action are grouped in pairs to cover all the possible relationships in which this love which is the fruit of the Spirit should be expressed. That is to say, there is not one single relationship which will not be affected by the presence of the Spirit in the heart. Our possible relationships are just three: to others, to God, and to ourselves.

Longsuffering and *gentleness* describe the action of love in our relationships with others. Longsuffering is the word when we are on the bottom, when someone else is dominating us and we cannot help ourselves. Then love is a passive manifestation, and we call it longsuffering. But longsuffering needs kindness. Some people suffer long because they cannot help themselves; they are not kind. Gentleness is the word when one is on top and has authority. Then love should express itself as gentleness.

Our relationship to God when we are under the Spirit's control will be love characterized by *faith* and *goodness.* We cannot speak of our relation to God without being theological. Faith and goodness are frequently pursued theologically in separation, instead of in the living synthesis which we are here being taught. It is proper to say that salvation is by faith. It is also proper to say that salvation is by goodness. When one says that salvation is a gift, quite independent of our good deeds, to be appropriated by faith, he speaks truth. The whole truth, however, requires that salvation produce actual goodness. Whatever we mean by salvation by faith it must mean a salvation which condones no sin, nor makes any room for evil. Righteousness, as the older theologians would have said, is not only *imputed* but also *imparted.*

While humility must not become a cloak for sin and defeat, it is also necessary that victory be witnessed to with a humility which excludes boasting and gives all glory to Christ. We need reminding again and again that the reality of our salvation does not depend upon our *feeling* saved. Salvation depends solely on the sacrifice of Jesus Christ. This is priceless, and to be witnessed to with thanksgiving and humility. The victory is not of ourselves nor of our fighting; it is the gift of God's grace. Therefore, to Him be all the praise! But that is not all. We make so many errors in judgment, say so many wounding words, give offense in so many ways, fail to pray as we ought, and are remiss in so many duties that even victory over known sin gives us nothing about which to boast. Moreover, often we are not even conscious of these weaknesses, at least not until after damage is done. Now these facts do not invalidate the sense of conscious victory. We are not to go around sad and introspective, refusing to claim any victory, merely for fear of what *might* have happened unwittingly or what may. The claiming of victory needs to be coupled with a deep understanding that the grace of God is constantly cleansing our souls of these inadvertent wrongs; and just as there is no specific consciousness of committing these wrongs, so is there no specific awareness of the cleansing. But that does not mean that either the wrongs or the cleansing are not there. And we ought to be wise to the facts and *consciously* give praise to God for what He is all the while doing and which we accept by faith. Our appreciation of grace and our humility of spirit should deepen as we realize how much God is having to do for us all the while we *feel* free from sin.

What then is to resolve the paradox of these two theological emphases, faith and goodness? It is love. Love holds the tension in equilibrium. Love is "the bond of perfectness" (Col. 3:14).

It is one of the queer facts of human nature that we have relations with ourselves; that we can, so to speak, hold ourselves off and look at ourselves, talk to ourselves, and manage ourselves. Indeed, our chief problem in life is usually our self. When, however, we have the fulness of the Spirit, He bears fruit as love in this relationship and it manifests itself in two directions: *meekness* and temperance, or *self-control.* Here is another living paradox — another tension between two poles maintained in the synthesis of love. Either of these poles taken alone is perilous.

At the heart of sanctification is an utter surrender. But it is more than a single act. Initiated as an act, it must be maintained as a condition. And a constant state of surrender is described for us here as *meekness.* There is a peril here, however, if we suppose that our condition is to be merely quiescent, motionless, static, and irresponsible. Meekness, or constant surrender, must be matched by a further conception. God accepts our surrender only to turn back to us our lives to hold as a trust in stewardship.

The proof of His acceptance of us is a gigantic act of faith on His part. He gives back all, asking that we render a faithful stewardship. Every part of our nature is capable of being used as an instrument of revolt. Any part may become a tool for dishonoring Him. And as we have seen, the line between stewardship for His glory and stewardship for the glory of self is so fine and crossed so unwittingly that only the faithful Voice of the Holy Spirit is sufficient safeguard against the wiles of the Devil here expressed. But God takes the risk. Loyalty on our part touches and satisfies within Him a very deep desire, and He rewards it with the huge trust of making us His stewards. He, therefore, does not take from us our self, but as we constantly yield it up He places it within our control as a stewardship forever. He does not take our tongues, but He expects us to govern them to His praise. He does not take away our sensitiveness, our hunger, our urges, our capacities, but He expects a reckoning someday of our use of them all. As the center of our gift to Him is self, stewardship of self becomes *self-control*. And that is the opposite pole from *meekness* in the tension of love which exists within the self.

Much has already been said about the discipline of the surrendered self. Something more needs to be said, however, about love as an emotion by way of keeping it in proper relation to action. Emotion is an essential part of any life and therefore it is not to be divorced from Christian experience. One can be sure that Christianity without emotion is not a living Christianity. Of course, the exercise of emotion requires discipline.

Emotion, reason, volition, instinct, or any other phase of life is dangerous when it is made an end in itself. Each, however, has an essential function to perform. The function of emotion is primarily to serve as a spring of action.

William James said in his classic writing on habit that it is harmful to submit to emotional experiences without giving them appropriate modes of expression in life. In illustration he said that if one listened to a concert which stirred him deeply he ought not be content merely to absorb the good feeling but should give expression to that feeling in some kind deed such as calling on one's grandmother the next day!

There is great danger that the emotional element in Christian experience shall be isolated and made an end in itself. This applies equally to philosophical mystics and to Holy Rollers. The former tend to define religion in terms of the quality of emotional experience, while the latter tend to define religion by the quantity of emotional or ecstatic expression. Both are right in so far as they emphasize the fact that emotion must have a place in life, but both are wrong in that they make that place an end in itself, failing to make emotion a spring of action in a total way of life. Undoubtedly, the emphasis on holiness in many circles has become terribly confused with extreme emotionalism. There are perils in emotionalism and they ought to be faced with frankness and discipline.

The first is the peril of losing sincerity in emotional form. There are people who are sure that until a certain outward emotional pitch is reached there is no blessing in a meeting. They feel that *every* meeting ought to run noisily along. They pray God loudly to smash the formality round about, without realizing that this style of praying may be a formal bondage. We have not always recognized the formalisms of informality. Those who judge that the Spirit is not free until the saints are whooping it up, ought to ask themselves whether there is not enough variety and spontaneity in the Spirit of God for Him occasionally to want to be quiet.

The second peril is that of seeking for emotional excitement instead of God. If in our finding God we find ourserves profoundly stirred and moved to immediate and ecstatic expression, well and good; but let us not seek the ecstasy as a road to God nor suppose that the ecstasy *is* God.

Another peril is that of adverse witness. This involves what others think — what impressions our emotionalisms make on others. A Christian ought to be gracious; and we have no right to parade our piety in ways which are an offense to the modesty or the sense of order and decency of good people. True it is that carnality parades in a cloak of respectability which dislikes being ruled, but it is not safe for us to rationalize our crudities by blaming the offended person for a lack of spirituality. It is possible that grace should make anyone able to stand any amount of torture, but it is not of grace that we should torture anyone. The Christian life should be a constant study in graciousness and we need in this matter to remember Jesus' condemnation of those who cause offense to others.

A still greater peril is that of wasted energy. The purpose of emotion is to be a spring of action. When one is stirred by a sermon, or is inspired in prayer, or is thrilled by singing, there ought to be a reservoir of energy that will find expression immediately afterward in Christian service — winning some soul, laboring in intercession, expressing some generosity in giving to the Lord's work or to the needy, visiting the sick or those in prison, helping the widow and orphan, cheering and giving companionship to the lonely, ministering the things of the Spirit, and the like. If this reservoir is expended habitually in emotional expression alone, Christian service will suffer and personal character will become flabby and sentimental. The wise Christian has a program of service at hand as an outlet for the emotions and as a discipline of them.

Discipline — or control — is the proper word, in spite of the tendency of many to measure spirituality by the amount of *abandonment* achieved. And here is the most subtle peril of them all. The heart of the experience of holiness is an utter, utter surrender to Christ. It is then a subtle snare of the enemy to confuse that surrender with emotional abandonment. The enemy loves to shift our attention from some vital matter with which God is having controversy and draw a false issue in some emotional demonstration. Perhaps there is a bad home relationship. This calls for surrender and a willingness to face it in the Spirit of Christ. It becomes easier, however, to cry and struggle and shout before sympathetic friends who will at the end of the paroxysm assure the person that he or she should now "take it by faith." The seeker then goes home with a sense of victory and assurance based upon having been willing to pay the price of making a scene, and he is troubled in heart the next day when in the midst of the home situation — still unresolved — the glow of victory fades.

If one presses this identification of surrender with emotional abandonment to its logical conclusion, it issues in a state where any remaining vestige of rational control over oneself seems to be by that much a lack of surrender. One then finds himself in a temporary period of abandonment where he is not his own and not responsible for his utterance or his conduct. That is why such action is plagued with so much moral breakdown and wreckage. Paul warns that the "spirits of the prophets are subject to the prophets" — not to an outside force — not even to God except as His power passes through the prophet's will. The final fruit of the Spirit is self-control.

Jesus is the perfect example of discipline. He wept over Lazarus but you cannot imagine Him wailing. He was happy with the children, with Mary and Martha, with His disciples, but can you imagine Him being frivolous? His joy was tempered by the sobriety of the impending Cross. Perhaps if there were more cross in our lives our joy would be more sober, deeper, and more genuine.

Among some Christians there is often to be found a deep uneasiness about emotional excesses, but a complete bondage to the same through a fear that any word of criticism or discipline would be to "quench the Spirit." But how many times the Spirit is quenched by unbridled emotional-

ism!   There is a clear call, especially to all the holiness
sects, to take this matter in hand with a discipline pleasing
to God.   At the other end of the scale, however, are those
who glibly assume that the holiness sects are composed of
mere fanatics and not worth serious advice — that they just
don't matter.   This is a real disease.   *There is absolutely
no one who does not matter to real love.*   Let those who
would hastily build a united church remember this!

But what of those who reject all but the severely classical
expressions of religious emotion?   Here are perils again
which are just as formidable as the perils of excess pointed
out above.

It is precisely because emotion is a spring of action and
in Christian experience a powerful prod through conscience
to moral living that many want their religion done up in
a capsule of icy formalism.   Here are those whose religion
is set about with stained glass, through whose Gothic tracery
merely enough light or warmth is permitted to enter to
minister a feeling of personal comfort but through which
no outlook upon the world's suffering is possible, nor sharp
ray of conviction of sin able to enter.

In the liturgical churches the emotional factor in worship
is placed under severe regulation.   The world's best artists
have been called upon to lay hold of the best architectural,
literary and musical forms, and no matter how humble the
worshiper, nor how lacking in artistic appreciation, he is
bound to use good art, for the church has seen to that.
But even in the field of secular art there are constantly recurring outcries against stereotyped forms and an insistence
that beauty can only be a thing of joy forever if an element
of spontaneity is maintained both in the work of the artist
and of the appreciator.   Non-liturgical churches have tried
hard to maintain this spontaneous element, without which
emotion dies.   Not always have they succeeded, for informal-
ism sometimes becomes formalism.   But the maintenance
of a living spontaneity is a necessity for true worship.

I have many times heard the sonorous phrases of the

Prayer Book read by hearts so sincere that it was as fresh as though it were an original outburst of a loving heart. But I have more often heard it read mechanically. It always sounds beautiful. But it does not always sound like worship. All depends upon the heart laying it under service. I will never forget hearing that saintly man of God, Bishop Abraham, late Metropolitan of the Mar Thoma Syrian Christian Church of Travancore, reciting the lengthy and involved liturgy of the communion before 5,000 communicants in the Cathedral at Maramon. Even in Malayalam, which I did not understand, I could feel the tremendous shepherd heart of this Indian saint going out through every phrase to God for his people. A clergyman all the while kept swinging a censor of incense towards us. The Anglican Bishop of Madras who was standing by my side in the chancel — we were guest speakers — afterward facetiously asked me what my Quaker friends would think if they knew I had been incensed! But somehow out of that service the incense and the vestments, the intoning and the ritual, and much else which is offensive to a simple Quaker have faded into the background, and in my memory stands out that splendid view of the man of God in utter sincerity truly worshiping in the media of tremendous liturgy. But the peril is there none the less. And the Mar Thoma Church, which awoke to a splendid evangelistic passion under its saintly Metropolitan, whose volunteer evangelists have been winning about a thousand Hindus to Christ annually for many years, is now under test to see whether it can maintain this spiritual life or whether it will be smothered by its ritual.

Since ritual so easily stifles spontaneity, many of us will choose spontaneity even at considerable cost. Where masses of uncultured people are touched by the Spirit of God, the manner of expression may be crude. This calls for teaching rather than censure. People can be led into more winsome expressions but they cannot be driven nor frozen into them. For the benefit of freedom and spontaneity, however, we shall have to be prepared to pay a certain price in lack of artistry, for the common people who hear Him gladly are not all artists unless there is something truly artistic in spontaneity itself.   When a young married woman just converted rose in a testimony meeting and said that the depression had worried her terribly (her husband was unemployed), but that since they had established a family altar she felt she could just say, "To the dickens with the depression," we all felt that back of the somewhat inelegant expression was a thing of beauty and real worth.   That thing was sincerity.   None of us had any doubt but that God had been immensely real in that woman's life and that she really meant what she said.

Paul uses the words *joy* and *peace* as descriptive of Christian feeling and one needs from the life of Jesus to add the word *compassion*.   Christian joy is realistic; it is no escape mechanism.   It is entirely consistent with the most sober facing of the starkest reality.   Peace is likewise a thing of sobriety, although a thing of joy.   Perhaps peace is the passive counterpart to active joy.   Peace and joy are ours as they were Christ's not as vapid sentiments, but as disciplined springs of action.   And when our peace and joy confront a suffering world they become compassion which drives us out upon the dusty highway in loving service.

"The joy of the Lord is your strength" (Neh. 8:12). Here is one of the most realistic verses in the Bible.   And one of the cleverest devices of the Devil is to rob a Christian of his joy.   With it goes his strength, and defeat is imminent. The joy of the Lord is something to be held at any cost. We cannot afford to let it go under any circumstance.   It does not disappear with suffering.   The joy of the Lord remains even in sorrow and is a sustaining portion.   It is strength.   Only self-centeredness can take away this joy.   If we find our joy slipping, we need quickly to search out and destroy that assertion of self, or that self-pity, which is driving out joy.   Nothing on earth is worth letting the joy of the Lord get away from us.   "In quietness and confidence shall be your strength" (Isa. 30:15). That is peace. Biblical peace and biblical joy are the emotions which every Christian needs.

Mere sentiment is cheap and safe. It always keeps itself protected. But love must act; it must express itself. One sees something of what I mean when he reads of the early Quakers who requested Parliament to allow them to enter prison in the place of other Quakers who were dying in those putrid dungeons.[2] In this, one sees love in action — that people should want to save the lives of their friends — but one sees something more when he learns that this request was motivated by an astounding desire to keep *blood guiltiness off the heads of the jailors!* Sentiment would have said, "Isn't it too bad about those folk who are dying in prison?"

Calvary is the love of God in action. May I suggest what a different thing it would have been if God had looked upon our miserable condition and merely pitied us! He could have commented on our plight with genuine feeling and regretted deeply the tragedy of the fall, done nothing, and still have been one of the great gods. But no John would have written, "God is love." But since He is really God, and since God *is* love, He could not look on, pitying but inactive. Being love, He could do no less than act for our redemption. By Calvary we *know* that He is love. And if the love of Christ possesses us, it must express itself in Calvary-like action.

There is a lesson to be learned from the woman who washed Jesus' feet with costly ointment. A wasteful act, said Judas, irregular and uncalculated. But Jesus approved of it because it was an expression of love. There is something extravagant about real love. The saints who impress us are not the devotees of sweet reasonableness, but the daring and prodigal lovers of Jesus.

2. George Fox, *Journal,* p. 307.